The
EVERYTHING.
Reading Music Book

Dear Reader,

Welcome, make yourself comfortable! I have wanted to write this book for a long time. Reading music is a subject that contines to amaze and fascinate me. It's also a subject that can confuse and intimidate others. The goal here is to enjoy making music. Music is one of the true gifts of life. It would be a shame to take that magic away with boring, intimidating language. My goal was to provide you with all the tools you need to read and understand music. This book broaches everything from simple pitches to advanced theory—everything you need.

It was also my goal to keep the material light, fun, and accessible to all. This was a true challenge—to speak to readers with such a wide array of musical backgrounds and still remain effective and enjoyable. The lessons learned here will give you the gift of music—share it with others. Don't ever think you're too old or "not the right type" to learn to read music. I didn't start reading music until I was eighteen years old. If I can, so can you. I hope you enjoy this book; it was an immense pleasure to share this with you.

Ciao,

Marc Sch

Welcome to the EVERYTHING® Series!

These handy, accessible books give you all you need to tackle a difficult project, gain a new hobby, comprehend a fascinating topic, prepare for an exam, or even brush up on something you learned back in school but have since forgotten.

You can choose to read an *Everything*® book from cover to cover or just pick out the information you want from our four useful boxes: e-questions, e-facts, e-alerts, and e-ssentials.

We give you everything you need to know on the subject, but throw in a lot of fun stuff along the way, too.

We now have more than 400 *Everything*® books in print, spanning such wide-ranging categories as weddings, pregnancy, cooking, music instruction, foreign language, crafts, pets, New Age, and so much more. When you're done reading them all, you can finally say you know *Everything*®!

QUESTIONS?
Answers to
common questions

FACTS
Important snippets
of information

ALERTS!
Urgent
warnings

ESSENTIALS
Quick
handy tips

PUBLISHER Karen Cooper

DIRECTOR OF ACQUISITIONS AND INNOVATION Paula Munier

MANAGING EDITOR, EVERYTHING SERIES Lisa Laing

COPY CHIEF Casey Ebert

ACQUISITIONS EDITOR Kate Powers

DEVELOPMENT EDITOR Brett Palana-Shanahan

EDITORIAL ASSISTANT Ross Weisman

Visit the entire Everything® series at *www.everything.com*

THE
EVERYTHING®
READING MUSIC BOOK

A step-by-step introduction to
understanding music notation and theory

Marc Schonbrun

Adams Media
Avon, Massachusetts

This book is dedicated to Joseph Mooney—Everything I know about music, you taught me. Thank you for the gift of my musical life.

An Everything® Series Book.
Everything® and everything.com® are registered trademarks of F+W Media, Inc.

Published by Adams Media, a division of F+W Media, Inc.
57 Littlefield Street, Avon, MA 02322 U.S.A.
www.adamsmedia.com

ISBN 10: 1-59337-324-4
ISBN 13: 978-1-59337-324-5
Printed in the United States of America.

20 19 18 17 16 15 14 13

Library of Congress Cataloging-in-Publication Data
Schonbrun, Marc.
The everything reading music book / Marc Schonbrun
     p.   cm.   (An Everything series book)
Includes bibliographical references.
ISBN 1-59337-324-4
1. Musical notation. 2. Sight-reading (Music) 3. Music theory–
Elementary works. I. Title. II. Series: Everything series.
MT35.S35 2005
781.4'23–dc22
2005009550

This book is available at quantity discounts for bulk purchases.
For information, please call 1-800-289-0963.

Contents

Space and Distance: Musical Intervals / 164

Vertical Thinking: Triads, Chords, Apeggios, and Seventh Chords / 177

Basic Harmony 101 / 194

Basic Major Scale Chord Progressions / 207

Advanced Chord Progressions / 219

Other Scales / 232

Acknowledgments

I need to thank: My family—Mom, Dad, Bill, Trish, and David. Doug Rubio, Paul Steinberg, Bret Zvacek, and David Heinick at The Crane School of Music for my wonderful education. Paul Siskind for his foreword and insightful comments. Frank Feldman, Eric Starr, and Kelly Moran for adding their talents to the audio CD. Steven Powell for the helpful KidSib font. Ron James for the Illustrator help. Sibelius software for perfect music notation software. And last, my patient wife who has endured yet another "crazed husband writing a book" phase: Without her help and support, I could not do this.

*CD Mastered by Barry Diament Audio, New York.
*No real pianos were harmed making this CD. (Not that I didn't try.)

Top Ten Things You Will Learn
From Reading This Book

1. How to read pitches, sharps, flats, and naturals.
2. How to read notes in every clef.
3. All about meter, key signatures, and time signatures.
4. How to count and subdivide rhythms.
5. How to interpret symbols and instructions in a score.
6. How to "spell" major, minor, harmonic, melodic, pentatonic, blues, chromatic, whole tone, diminished, and modal scales.
7. How to spell any chord or arpeggio imaginable.
8. Chord progressions.
9. The transposing instruments and how to transpose.
10. How to read a lead sheet/chord sheet.

Foreword

There are many paths that can lead to becoming an accomplished musician. Some people are born with natural ability, while others have to work hard to develop their skills. Some styles of music require years of formal training; others invite participation by amateurs with little training.

Music reading is a skill that fits into this broad continuum in a variety of ways. In some musical styles, you don't need to be able to read music to enjoy participating or to become moderately successful. In other styles, the ability to read music is an absolute necessity. However, no matter what musical style you favor, an ability to read music can greatly enhance your skills, your enjoyment, and your chances for success.

At the most basic level, music notation is a language, a way of communicating musical ideas and instructions. It is a very efficient language, much more efficient than having to learn things by trial-and-error, by ear, or by rote memorization. It also allows musicians from different styles to communicate across stylistic borders.

But the ability to read music is not only a practical aid to becoming a better performer; it also helps you to appreciate music more by understanding the inner workings of music. Music notation opens the door to music theory, which is simply the study of how music is put together. Music theory forms the core of understanding that all accomplished musicians share, and you cannot really excel as a musician without some understanding of theory. But theory is not only useful to practicing musicians; an understanding of theory can greatly increase the appreciation and enjoyment that you get from listening to music.

My experience as a teacher has shown that musicians generally fall into one of two broad categories of innate learning approaches: experiential or cognitive. Experiential musicians tend to learn by doing; they first master a skill, and then later understand the concepts behind what they're doing. Cognitive musicians tend to do the opposite; they first learn the concepts of what they're trying to do, and this understanding helps them to learn how to actually do the skill. Either type of learning approach can lead to success as a musician, regardless of the musical style. But good musicians of any type learn to develop both the experiential and cognitive approaches, because neither approach is effective by itself; experience leads to deeper understanding, and understanding helps improve practical ability. Thus, no matter what your natural learning approach is, and no matter what musical style you enjoy, you will be a better musician if you work to improve both the doing and the understanding of music.

As a subject, music theory can seem to be a daunting puzzle to some people. My hunch is that this often occurs when a student who has a high predilection toward experiential learning is taught by a book or teacher that takes a highly cognitive approach (or vice versa); the difference of approach can lead to frustration. Because of this, beginning music theory can be a surprisingly difficult subject to teach. It can be hard for accomplished musicians who have developed both their experiential and cognitive abilities to get beyond their own natural abilities and understand the areas that might not come naturally to different students.

But music theory doesn't have to be a difficult subject, if the teaching approach is tailored to properly connect with the students. In this book, Marc Schonbrun has succeeded in doing just that. There are many other books about music reading and basic theory available; most of these take a cognitive approach because they've been developed for high school and college classes, making them hard for some types of musicians to connect with. Marc does the opposite; his approach starts from your experience as a musician and listener, and builds up understanding of the concepts from your experiences. He gets you to the heavy stuff, but he eases you into it, rather than hitting you over the head with it. He accomplishes this in an approachable and easygoing manner. Musicians of many types will enjoy learning from Marc's creative approach to unlocking musical understanding.

Dr. Paul Siskind
Associate Professor, Crane School of Music, SUNY-Potsdam

Introduction

Close your eyes and turn on a CD. It can be anything you want, from Bach to the Beatles. Imagine that all the music you hear can be written down, preserved, and reproduced later, by strangers who have never heard the "real thing." The fact that music can go from the page to our ears is amazing. Everything from "Mary Had a Little Lamb" to Beethoven's majestic Fifth Symphony can be written down and replayed by musicians who read music. This is where you come in. Can you read music well? Can you read music at all?

Whether you learned to read music probably depends on what instrument you play. People who studied an instrument that was taught in school and continued from fourth or fifth grade upward probably read music well. They spent years, even if it was just once a week in a band or orchestra, reading music. All it took was time and some instruction. The same holds true for those who studied privately.

Large numbers of players are self-taught and don't interact with the music-reading universe. If you're self-taught, reading music may not have been in your own curriculum. Whether you're starting from square one or simply filling in the gaps, *The Everything® Reading Music Book* will help you read music better than you do now.

Music is a language all to itself. It has its own grammar and syntax just like English does. Unlike other languages you may have studied, music has its own symbols to learn; this is not unlike Russian, Arabic, and Hebrew languages that have new alphabets to learn. Music has the task of representing two main aspects: pitch and rhythm—what note and how long to hold it. It does so in a fairly simple way, using a linear system to represent music. Music has been around for a very long time, and music notation has been in existence since 800 B.C. Amazingly, little has changed since the 1600s—the system works just as well now as it did then.

This book focuses on three main areas: symbols, theory, and music as a whole. No matter how you slice it, you have to know what the symbols on a musical page signify—this is most of the task of reading music. This could be as simple as reading a single-line melody, or as complicated as changing a jazz "lead sheet" from fairly stark symbols to a living, breathing piece of music. After you are comfortable looking at and reading music on your instrument, the next step is to look at the system of music theory to see how musicians and composers have organized the various elements together into harmony, melody, scales, and chords. Knowing this will make you a better reader and a better musician.

Never lose sight of the goal: making music. In the end, being a better reader will allow you to make music as never before. Poor reading ability is akin to illiteracy in our society. You can "get by," but you will never succeed. It's the same way in music: Being a good reader will open doors for you. Through the study of pre-existing, familiar music, we will get a grasp on the entire breadth of written music, from the simple to the sublime. A side benefit of this study is that no matter how well you play or sing, the study of music and its underlying theory will make you a better musician—a better player. Who could argue with that? So whether you are a seasoned veteran looking to fill in the blanks or a longtime player, first-time reader, you will gain insight into music in a logical and orderly fashion. Let's get ready to learn everything about reading music!

Special Note about the CD

The first 35 examples relate to rhythm. On the CD, you will hear a snare drum bang out the examples. The CD is set up so that the drum is on one speaker and a metronome click is on the other. While this may seem odd at first, it will allow you to practice the examples with just the metronome click if you wish—just use the pan knob on your stereo to block out the snare or the metronome click. If you don't have a pan knob, use headphones and only use one headphone.

Chapter 1
The Written Note

Reading music entails learning another language—a written system that tackles the amazing challenge of translating sounds into two-dimensional globs of ink. For those who have never read music, this may seem scary—but have no fear; it's easy to get the hang of. Chapter 1 looks at where written music came from and how music has changed. Even if you have never read a note, this is the place to start.

Why Read Music?

No matter what your background is, you have picked up this book because you love music and you want to learn more about the systems that make it work. Reading music is one of the most important aspects of being a musician, yet many musicians cannot read music at all, and others only a little. The majority of good music readers got started through music lessons they took growing up. But not everyone learned music in an organized way or through an established method.

Being able to read music is not necessary to making music. Music is an art of the ears. Reading music is just a way of capturing and reproducing performances. There have been and will always be individuals with strong musical instincts who simply "play" instruments. The term playing by ear sums up this kind of learner. There will always be immensely talented folks who simply pick up instruments and, with no training and no reading ability, just play—and play well!

FACT

Certain instruments require less reading than others. Guitar has a very old system called tablature, which is a visual system of representing guitar parts in a very different way than other written music. Tablature still dominates guitar music and few guitarists can read standard written music. Vocalists often don't read because of the way that vocal music is taught: rote learning by listening to their parts played on piano negate the need to read anything but the lyrics.

If music is an art of the ears and in the end it's the final aural output that matters, why read music at all? There are many answers for this. First, while music may be an aural art, the language of writing it down and preserving it is important to understand the history and the evolution of music. Reading music is like literacy: You can survive somewhat in society without being able to read, but you'll never get a good job and you will miss out on many opportunities, no matter how smart you are. Many music teachers use this analogy, and it's valid. Second, this book is not just about "reading" music per se, it's also about all the information that you can learn when you have the ability to read music. Theory, scales, modes, arpeggios, composing, and arranging: all of these are tied into reading and documenting music. Reading music makes the entire universe of music available to you! Finally, the ability to read music will allow you to play and collaborate with a larger variety of musicians. Working with other players will expand your skill and, in the end, make you a better player. Isn't that what we all want—to make better music?

The Evolution of Written Music

What we see today as "typical" music notation appears to look nothing like it did when music first began to be notated. However, very little has changed and there are constants that are still around today. The earliest written music dates back to 800 B.C. (more than 2,800 years ago!). In early written music, small dots, or neumes as they are called in this style of notation, signify the name of the note that is played. Different shaped neumes correspond to different rhythmic values in the music. The one thing that is consistent in all written styles of notation is the concept of "vertical sound." Music has high and low notes; this is something that everyone can perceive just by listening. Since written music is a graphical representation of sound, the higher notes sit higher vertically on the staff than the lower notes. This makes just good sense!

Music has gone through some important changes since 800 B.C., but it hasn't changed all that much since it was standardized in the fifteenth century. The vertical system for showing pitch hasn't changed. Rhythms are indicated now more exactly than they were then. However, the same basic information is present then and now; the only difference is what symbols are in standard use today.

Pitch is one-third of what written music communicates. Another third of the puzzle is rhythm, or how long a note is sustained (or not sustained, as indicated by a rest). Rhythm hasn't changed, but the symbols used to show rhythm have changed over time. We have standardized a system of rhythm that is clean and easy to understand. If we were to stop there with just notes and rhythms, we would have a fairly effective means of communicating music. We can go one step further and add the final piece of the puzzle: dynamics and expression. This final category covers everything else that defines music: the degree of loud or soft, different sound colors, particular ways of playing, tempo and tempo changes. **FIGURE 1-1** is a short example to show you a standard piece of music.

FIGURE 1-1   Modern Notation Example

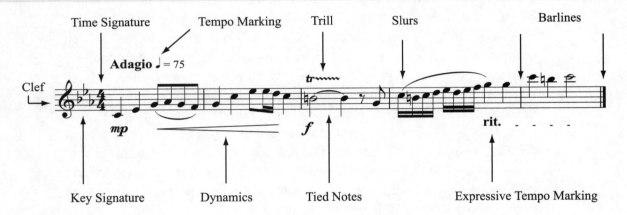

As you can see on the music and its corresponding labels, music can be broken down into very simple and easy-to-understand sections. It may look confusing now, but you'll soon learn what all of these symbols mean. Just remember that what written music tells you—what note to play and how long to play it—is fairly simple. The details will come later.

Who Reads Music?

The question "Who reads music?" would seem a bit obtuse—doesn't every instrument read the same music? Sure, every instrument does, but there are some generalizations about certain instruments and their proclivity toward reading. Many of the greatest musical jokes have been based on vocalists' and guitarists' inability to read music. In general, those who read music are usually trained. It is certainly possible for someone to learn to read music all on his or her own, but this is not often the case. Reading music is a skill and a language all by itself. Practice or repetition is the key to making it work. Reading music is a language that anyone can learn. All you have to do is start.

Why Would You Want To?

What benefits will you gain by learning more about music? Put simply, being able to read music opens new doors. For example, many enjoy relaxing by reading a new book. Books offer stimulation and relaxing enjoyment. Why not sit down and read music? Dive into some of the greatest music ever composed! If you rely on your ear and recordings for your music, you are limited to the history of recordings, which are a mere 100 years old or so. There are some amazing teachers who are long dead that you can study with if you know how to read their incredible legacy of written music. The amount of music that exists in written form is staggering. It's more than you can imagine! There is so much to learn, study, and just simply enjoy about music.

Don't Shut Yourself Out

If you have ever thought about a career in music, or simply making music on the semi-professional level, then solid reading skills are essential. When it comes to collaborating with other musicians, especially rewarding work like duet, trio, and chamber groups, you will have to read music. A lot of this depends on the musical culture that you live in. Many musicians who can't read play popular music styles where reading music isn't essential. For example, it's very common to have a rock or pop band full of nonreaders. The music is learned through aural tradition passed from one member to the next, or in the case of piano, guitar, and bass, chord symbols and lead sheets predominate over standard written music. (You'll learn more about lead sheets in Chapter 20.)

Different Instruments Read Different Music

Is written music truly universal for all instruments? Well, yes and no—it depends on the instrument and what it's reading. Compare the examples shown in **FIGURES 1-2, 1-3,** and **1-4**.

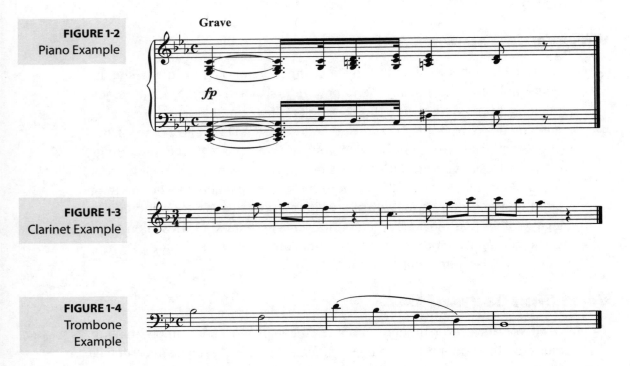

FIGURE 1-2
Piano Example

FIGURE 1-3
Clarinet Example

FIGURE 1-4
Trombone Example

Are these the same? What do you observe? For starters, the system of notes on the staffs is the same. Notes indicate pitch and rhythm. Notes sit on five-line staffs, yet there are some very different things going on in each of these examples. Could the trombone player read (and play) the piano part? Not really. The piano plays more than one note at a time and a trombone does not. Could the clarinet play the trombone part? No, as clarinet and trombone play different ranges of notes, represented by different clefs (indicated by the symbols at the beginning of each staff). Every detail is explored later in the book, but you can see that music can be very instrument-specific. For instance, piano reads two staffs at once, while most other instruments read only one at a time. Certain instruments read in certain clefs and some transpose. These are all things that are specific to the instrument that you play.

The general parts about reading music are just that—general! The specifics of your own instrument will always complicate the issue. This book will try to address the specifics of individual instruments—but it is not a substitute for methods and manuals that train you to play a particular instrument. Studying music symbology here will make your experience using any other music book easier and more rewarding.

The Different Forms of Written Music

There is more than just one way to communicate music in written form. We have just seen "standard" examples of staffs of music. These can be combined into larger groups for symphonies or reduced for one-line solos. Yet this is not the exclusive way to write music. Tablature, lead sheets, and chord chart notation are viable alternatives to standard pitched music. Let's explore each briefly.

Tablature

Tablature—or tab, as it's commonly referred to—is an alternate form of notation that is commonly used for guitar and bass. **FIGURE 1-5** shows an example of guitar tablature.

FIGURE 1-5 Guitar Tab Example

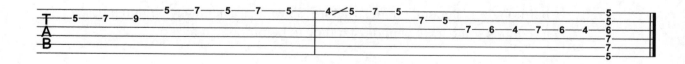

Guitar tab is specific to the guitar; other instruments cannot read this notation. The six horizontal lines represent the six strings of the guitar, while the numbers indicate which fret to press down. Rhythms are typically excluded. This is one of the major weaknesses of tablature. Tablature dates back to Renaissance times. Back then, rhythm was indicated above the staff, so the tablature were musically more complete than they are now. Tab is not exclusively used for strings; harp commonly uses visual tablature to indicate harp pedaling. However, it is much more common with guitar.

Lead Sheets

A lead (pronounced "leed") sheet is common musical shorthand to indicate a song via a single written melody and chord symbols. **FIGURE 1-6** is an example of a lead sheet.

FIGURE 1-6   Lead Sheet

A lead sheet is more of a skeleton than anything else. The players are able to decipher the basic sheet and turn it into music. For example, the melody would be sung or played by an instrument. The bass could play the roots of the written chords (example: C for a C chord) and the piano or guitar player play the chords written above the melody. Percussion and drums would simply improvise a part that fit. This is the standard way for jazz music and other popular styles to represent music. What's unique about a lead sheet is that only one part of the music is written in standard notation: the melody. In order to play the other parts, you need to know something about music, harmony, and general chord structure. So while it's definitely written music, it requires some level of understanding to be properly realized.

Chord Charts

Chord charts are a variant on lead sheets and are typically used for instruments such as guitar, piano, autoharp, and any other instrument capable of playing chords. Instead of writing chords out note-by-note, symbols are given for the chords in shorthand. What is different about chord charts compared to lead sheets is that the duration of the chords is notated with standard rhythmic notation. **FIGURE 1-7** shows an example.

FIGURE 1-7   Chord Chart

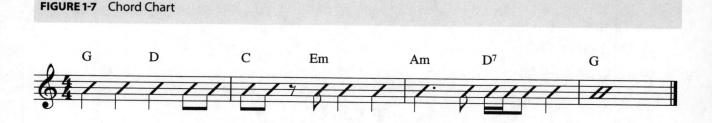

This type of notation is common for jazz, pop, and show music. If you read a harmonic instrument (piano or guitar), expect to see this often. Again, this form of written music presupposes some basic knowledge of chords. One of the cool things about chord symbols is that there is an element of improvisation involved. The written music does not tell the player exactly how to play the chord. The player will realize the chords as he sees fit, so each performance varies slightly.

Digging In

We have briefly gleamed over each basic style of notation without going into too much detail. We have laid some groundwork, but the purpose of this book is to be complete and thorough—so with that in mind, let's start from square one! If you have some background in reading music, don't immediately skip over this introductory material. It will be helpful to go over it once more to get a solid understanding. Though few take the time to learn the theory of reading music, it's often a stepping-stone to playing an instrument. Take your time and dig in. There is much to learn. Let's do it!

Chapter 2
The Elements

Music is a system like any other language—it consists of symbols and a method to organize them: grammar. Let's start cracking away so that you can look at any piece of music and say with confidence, "I know what that means." It will take you a bit of time to become a confident and comfortable reader, but there is no greater feeling than understanding what you're looking at.

Pitch

One of the most fundamental elements that music has to convey is pitch. Pitch is best defined as the sound of a note. There are more grandiose definitions that include talk of frequency and time (concepts from physics); however, it's much simpler to state that pitch is the name of the note that you play on your instrument. Music conveys this information by placing notes on a grid called a staff. This is the first element you need to understand, as the staff is the place where the notes live. The staff also serves as a visual reference—an easy way to organize the placement of notes.

The Staff

The staff is something to be marveled at. Simple, yet really effective. Without further ado, let's look at a staff, which is also commonly called a "stave"!

A staff (**FIGURE 2-1**) is nothing more than five lines grouped together. The result is a "home" for the notes. A staff provides five lines and four spaces for notes to live on. It provides not only a clean interface for the music but also an easy visual system for music. Notes are placed within the staff, either within the spaces or through the lines themselves. Notes that live lower on the staff vertically sound lower than notes that live on higher parts of the staff. This is the most basic concept in music: the height of sound. As a note visually climbs up the staff, its pitch rises. You'll see this clearly throughout the rest of the book. But how do you identify each note? Without understanding the musical alphabet, the staff won't mean much to you.

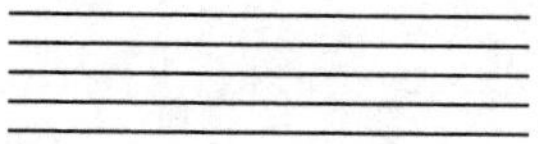

FIGURE 2-1
The Staff

The Musical Alphabet

Every note that you can play on an instrument can be named, just like a color on a color wheel. Music uses a standardized system of seven letters to name pitches.

The musical alphabet uses these letters: A B C D E F G. After G it cycles back to A every time. This can be a hard concept for many because music has so many sounds that seven letters couldn't possibly cover it. In truth, there are twelve, not just seven, but the extra five come from placing sharps and flats (discussed later in this chapter) in front of the notes. Even at twelve notes, it's still a remarkably efficient system.

On a piano's keyboard, A B C D E F G corresponds to the white keys. **FIGURE 2-2** shows an example of the notes on the piano.

FIGURE 2-2   Piano Keyboard

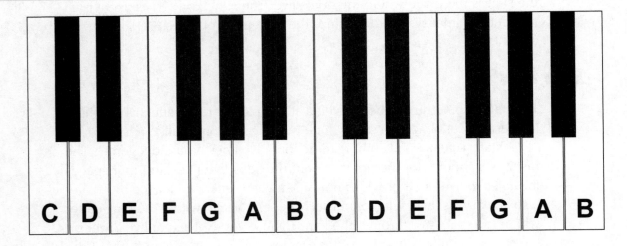

As you can see, the piano is a repeating visual pattern. Notice the pattern: three black keys, then two black keys. This repeats up and down the keyboard. This follows along with the rules of music. There are only twelve notes, which repeat throughout music. Each section of the piano is nothing more than identical groupings of twelve keys laid out left to right—this is done seven times across the piano. However, to identify any of these keys, the only letters you need to know are A B C D E F G. That's it!

Staffs Defined

So far, all you know is that a staff contains five lines and four spaces. How do you know where the note A or the note C is? By itself, a staff is a dead thing, nothing more than five lonely lines and four solemn spaces. The missing element needed is the clef. The clef defines what notes go where, a lot like a map. Clefs are covered in more detail later in this chapter. For now, let's just look at the treble clef to give some meaning to our staff.

Placing a treble clef at the start of the staff defines the lines and spaces with note names. **FIGURE 2-3** shows the notes of a treble staff.

FIGURE 2-3
Treble Staff

The treble clef circles around the note G. This is why it is commonly called the G clef. As for the notes, there is an important pattern. Look at the lowest line, which is designated E. Follow the musical alphabet to find where the next note is. The F is in the space just above the E. The staff ascends in this fashion, line then space then line, as it cycles through the musical alphabet. This is a crucial concept to understand.

The treble clef is one of a few clefs used in music. The different clefs, covered later in this book, rename the lines and spaces differently. The treble clef is a standard common clef that many instruments read. Some of the instruments that read the treble clef are

- Trumpet
- Clarinet
- Violin
- Saxophone
- Guitar
- Piano—the pianist's right hand

There is a great acronym to help you learn the names of the notes on the treble staff. This has been taught for generations! The notes that sit on the five lines make this phrase if we take the letters on the staff from bottom to top and make a sentence with them: Every Good Boy Does Fine. (See **FIGURE 2-4.**) The first letter of each word corresponds with the note name on the lines. Remembering this phrase is a great way to help you remember the note names rather than simply memorizing them by rote.

FIGURE 2-4 Staff Lines

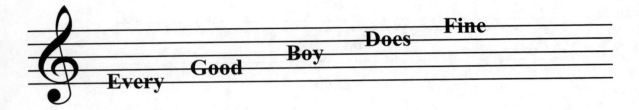

That takes care of the lines. Here are the spaces: From bottom to top, the notes spell the word FACE. (See **FIGURE 2-5**.) No acronym here, just a simple word that's also easy to remember.

FIGURE 2-5 Staff Spaces

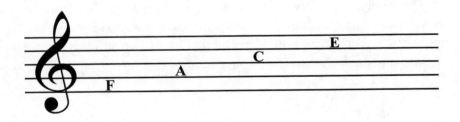

There are other clefs to investigate, but the treble clef is used so often that it's worth memorizing this trick, even if you play an instrument that reads in one of the other clefs.

Much of theory and many theory examples and simple melodies will be written in the treble clef, so get to know it well.

Identifying Notes

You're on a roll now. You've learned some of the most important concepts you need to be a successful music reader: clefs, the musical alphabet, and the staff. This is all well and good, but without notes, you're stuck. Notes, in their most basic sense, are simply sounds waiting to be played. A note is a small circle that is placed on a staff. **FIGURE 2-6** is a short example of a few notes placed on the treble staff. The names of the notes are written below.

FIGURE 2-6 Sample Notes

E   B   A   C   E

Notes can take many shapes and forms, but the most important thing is where they are on the staff; their location on the staff tells you the name of the note, or pitch as it is called. No matter what the notehead looks like—closed circle, open circle, etc.—if it's on the top space of the treble staff, it's the note E, no exceptions. Amazingly enough, that's almost everything you need to know about naming notes on the staff. Well, almost everything—the missing element of rhythm will be covered in Chapter 3. Rhythm further defines the appearance of the notes; it does not change their location.

Multiple Notes at Once

Music is read in a left-to-right fashion, just like English. You read notes in succession as you see them. The speed at which the notes progress depends solely on the rhythm and time signature, topics that are covered in Chapter 3. However, there is another important element you need to know: the appearance of multiple notes at once. When notes are stacked vertically, directly on top of each other, they are supposed to be played at the same time. For many instruments this is impossible, as they can only play one note at a time. For instruments such as piano, guitar, and the other chordal instruments, vertical groups of notes are common. **FIGURES 2-7** and **2-8** show two examples of stacked notes.

FIGURE 2-7 Stacked Notes

FIGURE 2-8
More
Stacked
Notes

In **FIGURE 2-8**, you'll notice that there are a few notes hanging off to the side of the otherwise perfect vertical stack. When the groupings of notes intersect on the staff because they are too close together, it's necessary to hang the note right alongside the other notes. It may look like that note is orphaned, but this is just to avoid smashing the notes together. When you come upon an example like **FIGURE 2.8**, play the notes all together.

Extending the Staff: Ledger Lines

The staff yields five lines and four spaces. That gives us a total of nine notes. Surely, there must be more than nine notes! Of course there are more than nine notes. The staff is just a home base; it can be extended up or down with the use of ledger lines. A ledger line is simply an extra line or lines above or below the staff to accommodate higher or lower notes. Unlike the normal five lines of the staff, ledger lines are only as long as the note they are attached to. Let's take a look at how we can extend the staff with some ledger lines (see **FIGURE 2-9**).

FIGURE 2-9 Ledger Line Examples

Ledger lines simply extend the notes when needed. The sixth or seventh line is not added permanently; it's just there when it's needed. Ledger lines can go as high as the sky, but they do get harder to read the higher and lower they go. Most folks like to read within the staff, and, thankfully, most instruments read many of their notes within the staff.

Ledger lines follow the same system of lines and spaces. Notes can sit either on the lines or in the spaces. You cycle through the musical alphabet the same way you did on the staff. This is handy in the cases where you encounter a rogue note above or below the staff and you have no idea what it is—simply count up or down from the last note you are sure you know the name of. If you encounter these notes often, you will learn them quickly.

Defining Clefs

Clefs define what the notes on the staff are called. The word clef comes from the French word for key, which is fitting, as it's the key to understanding what the notes mean. Without a clef at the start of the staff, nothing identifies what the second line or third space is. You looked briefly at the treble clef in the last section; now let's go further into treble and the other common clefs. Different instruments read in different clefs and some even read in more than one. No matter what you play, you should know the notes in the two most basic clefs: treble and bass clef.

The Treble Clef

The treble clef is a common clef and is usually used for higher pitched instruments, such as flute, clarinet, trumpet, and the piano's right hand. Treble is defined as the highest part of music, so the treble clef is used for the higher sounds. Historically, the treble clef has also been called the G clef because its unusual symbol grew out of a highly stylized script G. The symbol for the G clef also curves around the second line, which denotes the note G as well. **FIGURE 2-10** shows the mighty G, or treble, clef and the notes that it defines.

FIGURE 2-10 Treble or G Clef

The Bass Clef

The bass clef covers all of the lower sounds of music by defining many of the lower notes in music. The bass clef is also called the F clef because it resembles a stylized F. The bass clef symbol also is called F because the two dots surround the line F. **FIGURE 2-11** shows the bass clef and the notes that it defines in its lines and spaces. Notice that these notes are different than on the treble clef. Many of the lower instruments read in bass clef, such as string bass, cello, tuba, trombone, and the piano's left hand.

FIGURE 2-11 Bass or F Clef

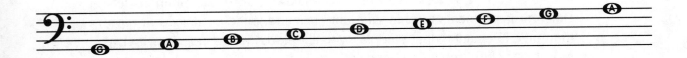

The Grand Staff

When you combine the bass and treble staffs together, you get something called the grand staff. The grand staff is read by pianists, as the piano has such a large range that it needs both clefs to cover the wide range of sounds. A grand staff combines two staffs, treble clef on top and bass clef on a separate staff below it, attached with a brace or a bracket (see **FIGURE 2-12**). The grand staff also lets you see just how the low and the high notes connect.

FIGURE 2-12 The Grand Staff

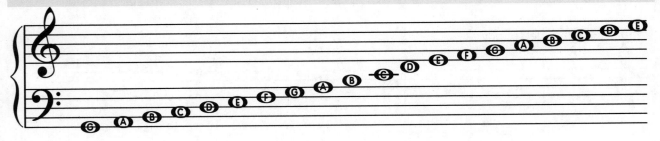

Notice how the note names start on the bottom of the bass clef and work their way up to the top of the bass clef? There is a ledger line between the two clefs. Is that ledger line above the bass clef, or is it below the treble clef? The answer is that it's both: The same note is one ledger line above bass staff and one ledger line below the treble staff. This is the point at which the two staffs join and cross; it's also called middle C. It also illustrates to you just how much higher the treble clef is than the bass clef (and how much lower the bass clef is than the treble clef). Understanding how the grand staff is connected is crucial to reading music.

Other Clefs

There is one more clef to look at, but before we do, we should look at the reasons for all these different clefs. Wouldn't it be easier just to read one clef for everyone? To help you understand why music bothers with two clefs, look at **FIGURES 2-13** and **2-14**. **FIGURE 2-13** shows a simple melody written in treble clef. But if you wanted the exact same melody played in the bass clef, it would look like **FIGURE 2-14**. Which would you rather read? Different clefs move the pitches so that the majority of the notes stay on and around the staff. It is difficult to read multiple ledger lines. Having different clefs makes them easier to read.

FIGURE 2-13   Treble Clef Melody

FIGURE 2-14   Bass Clef Melody

There is one last clef that you need to know about: the C clef, or alto clef. It's far less common than the other two, but is still used in modern music. The C clef resembles two Cs facing backward, fused together. Take a look at the good old C clef in action in **FIGURE 2-15**.

FIGURE 2-15   C Clef

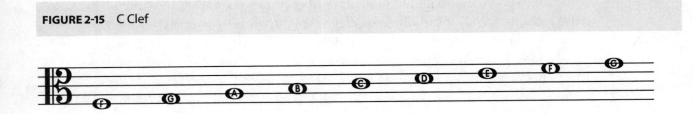

The trick with the C clef is that the clef has a little notch in the center of the clef. In the example, that notch sits on the middle line. Wherever that notch sits is where middle C is.

This clef is what a viola, and sometimes a trombone in its high register, usually reads.

If you compare the location of middle C on the alto clef to the bass or treble clef, you see that it's a bit higher than bass clef and a bit lower than treble clef—somewhere in the middle. That's precisely where the viola is, right in the middle. So this clef is perfect for keeping the majority of the viola's notes on and around the staff where they are easily read. Other than for viola and sometimes trombone, the C clef is far less common than the treble or the bass clef.

Accidentals

To this point, you have been reading about the "natural" notes, A B C D E F G, which correspond to the white keys on the piano. But there are other important musical symbols and, more importantly, other notes on the piano: the black keys. The piano serves as a great example for theory since it's so visual in nature. The term accidental is used for any pitch that is not natural, or on a white key. Accidentals take the form of sharps or flats.

Sharps, Flats, and Naturals

A sharp, denoted by the symbol ♯, raises any note up to the next highest key—to the right, if you use the piano as a guide. Find the C on the piano; the black key directly to the right of it is called C♯. The music to denote that key looks like **FIGURE 2-16**.

FIGURE 2-16   Example of a Sharp

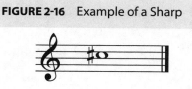

FIGURE 2-17   Double Sharps

The next level of sharps is called the double sharp. This "sharps" the note twice—raising it two keys to the right on the piano. A double sharp is designated by the symbol ✗ (see **FIGURE 2-17**). C✗ actually takes you to the same place as the note D, which may seem confusing, but there are valid reasons for all the strange musical rules! Later in the book you'll fully understand. You're not going to be barraged with double sharps, so don't worry too much.

A flat is the opposite of a sharp. Whereas a sharp raises any note up, a flat does the opposite: It lowers the note one key to the left on the piano. Flats use the symbol ♭ before any note that receives the flat. Let's go back to the piano for this example and play a D♭ (see **FIGURE 2-18**).

Simply go to the D and lower the note to the black key to the left of the D. Instant D♭. You can flat any note this way. And just like sharps, you can double flat any note. The symbol for double flat is ♭♭ (see **FIGURE 2-19**), and it is simply two flats together, moving the note two keys to the left.

FIGURE 2-18   Example of a Flat

FIGURE 2-19   Double Flat

ALERT!

Don't forget about the natural half steps! C♭ and F♭, E♯ and B♯ take you from white keys to white keys. This is a notable exception to the rule—keep it in mind.

A natural sign cancels out an earlier sharp or a flat sign and reverts the note back to its normal "natural" state, or white key on a piano. The sign for a natural is ♮ . Naturals are pretty straightforward. **FIGURE 2-20** shows a natural in written music. When would you use a natural? It's time to learn how accidentals affect other keys.

FIGURE 2-20
Example of a
Natural

The Key Signature

Accidentals, such as flats and sharps, can be placed in something called a key signature. A key signature indicates that one or more notes should be sharp or flat throughout the entire piece. This saves having to indicate an accidental that repeats often in the piece every time it comes up. Key signatures appear directly after the clef (see **FIGURE 2-21**).

FIGURE 2-21   Key Signatures

Key signatures are covered in greater detail in Chapter 10, but for now, here are a few quick things you should know about key signatures.

- There is a system that determines which notes may appear and in what order they may appear.

- When a note is altered in a key signature (such as marking a sharp for the note of E), every pitch that has the same name is affected—regardless of where it is on the staff (high or low).
- Key signatures are easier to read than many accidentals in written music.
- Signatures are composed of either flats or sharps, never mixtures of the two.

Measures and Accidental Precedence

We aren't going to get into the concept of a measure until the next few chapters, where it's closely tied with rhythm and meter. But there is no way to fully explain accidentals without talking about measures. A measure is simply a way of organizing groups of notes together into convenient little chunks. You'll learn later just how convenient they are, but for now, they are just ways to organize and group notes together. Measures are the result of bar lines (**FIGURE 2-22**) placed vertically on a staff, breaking the staff into regions. The bar line at the middle of the staff broke the otherwise long line into two parts, or measures as they are called in music. The terms measure and bar can be used in place of one another—they mean the same thing.

FIGURE 2-22 Bar Lines

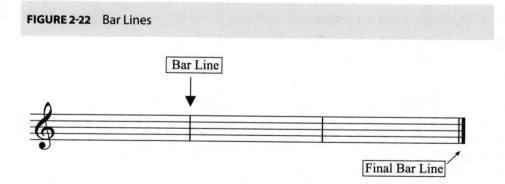

Measures are critical to understanding accidentals because an accidental is active for the entire measure it appears in. In real terms, if you see a C♯ at the beginning of a measure and several other Cs after the initial C♯, those Cs are assumed to be sharp; they will remain sharp until the start of the next measure, which is indicated by a bar line. Once the new measure starts, all of the previous accidentals are reset back to normal. If the music writer wanted another C♯ in the next measure, it would be indicated with a new sharp sign. **FIGURE 2-23** shows you how this works in real music.

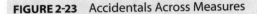

FIGURE 2-23   Accidentals Across Measures

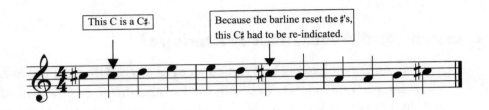

This is something that is easy to miss and easy to get wrong when you're first sight-reading music. Just remember, once you change any note to sharp, flat, or natural, it stays that way until the next bar and does so without having to be indicated again.

Natural signs are needed to cancel accidentals, which last for the whole measure. If you sharp a note at the beginning of a measure and you need to go back to its natural state, you need to indicate to the musician what to play. If you don't indicate a natural when you want it played, it's assumed to stay altered unless you say so. Naturals also cancel out accidentals in key signatures (see **FIGURE 2-24**).

FIGURE 2-24   Naturals Canceling an Accidental

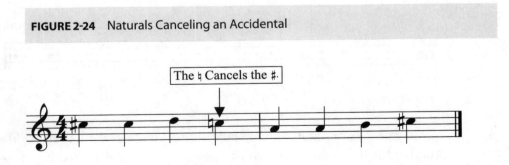

Enharmonics

There are twelve notes in music. While a piano has 88 keys, there are only twelve discrete pitches; they just keep repeating higher and lower with the same names. If you were paying close attention when learning about sharps and flats, you may have noticed that something strange occurred. The first example was C♯—the black key just to the right of the C on the piano. The next example was D♭—the black key just to the left of D on your piano.

If you played these, did you notice anything odd? C♯ and D♭ sound the same! Yes, that's right. They are exactly the same key. And it's not just the piano; for every instrument, C♯ and D♭ sound the same. Welcome to the world of enharmonics. Simply put, every black key on the piano has two names. Look at the list:

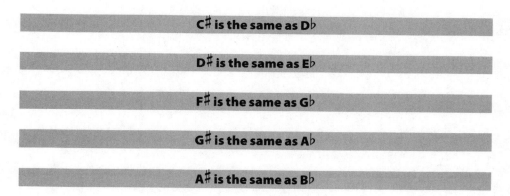

C♯ is the same as D♭

D♯ is the same as E♭

F♯ is the same as G♭

G♯ is the same as A♭

A♯ is the same as B♭

As to the greater question of which one to use and why, the simplest answer is that it depends on the piece of music. Usually readers like to see all sharps or all flats. So, if there is one flat in the music, the rest of the accidentals will also be indicated as flats. This will be covered in greater depth throughout the rest of this book. For now, just wrap your brain around the concept that C♯ and D♭ are considered different notes, yet they sound exactly the same. Now you're ready to move on to another fundamental aspect of written music—notating rhythm.

Chapter 3

Beat It: Rhythm

Rhythm is one of the main elements of music. Many argue that it has been around longer than pitch. Rhythm is a unique topic that is often overlooked and commonly misunderstood. Music organizes rhythm with meter and time, all of which are abstract concepts—but they don't need to be. Rhythm is one of the most fundamental aspects of music; you can feel rhythm. Now, learn to read and reproduce it on paper.

Components of Rhythm

Music is composed of pitch and rhythm. While there are finer elements that come into play later on, such as dynamics and expression, music can be made by knowing simply this: which note and how long to hold it. The last chapter explained how pitch is represented with notes, staffs, and clefs. But without rhythm, people couldn't fully read music.

Rhythm is music's way of setting the duration of a note. Music accomplishes this task by varying the appearance of the notes that sit on the staff. Different rhythms indicate different note lengths. To get us rolling, we need to speak about an essential concept: beat. Have you ever been to a concert and clapped along with 30,000 other fans? Have you ever noticed how everyone claps together in a steady pattern? Did you ever wonder how 30,000 people could possibly agree on anything? Have you been to a dance club and noticed that there is always a steady drumbeat or bass line to drive all club music along? Have you ever noticed that it's usually steady and rarely ever slows down? Those are all examples of pulse and beat in music. Rhythm is a primal element and pulse and beat are universal concepts.

ESSENTIAL

A device called a metronome can best illustrate what a steady pulse sounds like. Metronomes have one job—to sound a steady click. Metronomes are either mechanical and swing a weight back and forth to keep time or they are electronic and keep time using a battery and an audible chirp. The click becomes your beat and pulse. A metronome will never get tired and never waver. All serious music students should have one.

Basic Rhythms

In music, changing the appearance of the notes indicates the rhythm. As you will remember, the location of the notes is fixed on the staff, which will never change. The appearance of the note varies, indicating how long that note should be held. Let's start with the simplest rhythms first.

The first examples show the rhythms without a normal five-line staff. Instead, they use a single line and a universal clef. When you practice these examples, you can tap on a table, or play any note on your instrument. The goal here is to focus on rhythm. Wherever you are, simply tap on your leg eight times with your hand. Try to make the beats all evenly spaced and equal length (think of clapping at a concert). What you tapped out should look like the rhythm shown in **FIGURE 3-1**.

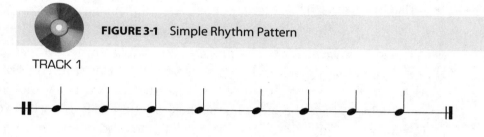

FIGURE 3-1   Simple Rhythm Pattern

TRACK 1

Quarter Notes

A quarter note ♩, which is signified with a filled-in black circle (also called a notehead) and a stem, is the simplest rhythm to talk about. Quarter notes receive one count; their duration is one beat (see **FIGURE 3-2**). A quarter note corresponds to every click on the metronome. To most people, quarter notes sound "steady" and regular.

FIGURE 3-2   Quarter Note

♩   Quarter Note = One Beat

FACT

Many notes have stems. The direction of the stem, either up or down, does not change the rhythmic value. Stems face up or down depending on where on the staff they are placed—notes low on the staff get "up" stems, notes high on the staff get "down" stems.

Half Notes

The next in our series of simple rhythms is the half note ♩. As you can see, the half note looks similar to the quarter note, except the circle is open and not filled in. Like a quarter note, it also has a single stem that points either up or down. The half note receives two counts; its duration is two beats. In relation to the quarter note, the half note is twice as long because it receives two counts (see **FIGURE 3-3**).

FIGURE 3-3   Half Note

Half Note = Two Beats

The easiest way to count half notes is to establish a steady beat in your hand, or by tapping your foot in a steady rhythm. Count to yourself: one, two, one, two. Every time "one" comes back around, you'd play another half note. It helps to have the metronome click or to tap your foot while you do this. **FIGURE 3-4** is an exercise combining half notes and quarter notes to help you feel the difference. The counting below the notes will help you keep track of where you are.

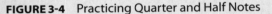

FIGURE 3-4   Practicing Quarter and Half Notes

TRACK 2

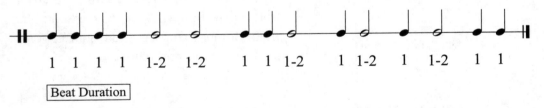

1   1   1   1   1-2   1-2   1   1   1-2   1   1-2   1   1-2   1   1

Beat Duration

Whole Notes

A whole note is a rhythm that receives four beats. It's twice as long as a half note and four times as long as a quarter note—count to yourself: one, two, three, four. It is represented as an open circle without a stem. The whole note is the single longest rhythmic value that you are likely to come

FIGURE 3-5 Whole Note

○ Whole Note = Four Beats

across (there are some ways to extend a whole note, which will be covered later). Whole notes are easy to spot because they are the only notes that lack a stem. (See **FIGURE 3-5**.)

FIGURE 3-6 is an exercise using quarter, half, and whole notes to help you practice these different rhythms. No matter how you practice rhythm, you're going to need to count the beats as you play them. Even professional musicians count along with the music at all times. It's something that you may feel weird doing at first. With some time, it will become a natural part of your playing.

FIGURE 3-6 Practicing Quarter, Half, and Whole Notes

TRACK 3

More Advanced Rhythms

Quarter, half, and whole notes provide the most basic rhythms in music. Mastering these basic beats sets a good foundation for you to build upon. The next step is to learn about the more advanced rhythms and techniques for dealing with more advanced rhythmic music. With some patience and a few batteries for your metronome, you should be good to go.

Eighth Notes

The smallest rhythm you have encountered thus far is the quarter note, which lasts for one beat. Chopping up this beat into smaller divisions allows musicians to explore faster rhythms and faster passages. Chopping the quarter note in half gives us the eighth note, which receives half of one beat (see **FIGURE 3-7**).

FIGURE 3-7 Eighth Notes

♪ Single Eighth Note = 1/2 of a Beat　　　♫ Two Eighth Notes Together = One Beat

Visually, eighth notes look similar to quarter notes, except that the end of the stem has a flag. This flag can take two forms. A single eighth note looks like ♪. When two or more eighth notes appear together, their flags join each other to look like this: ♫. The eighth notes are connected by a beam. Eighth notes can be grouped together in many ways; you'll learn more about this in Chapter 5.

Counting eighth notes is a bit trickier than counting quarter, half, or whole notes. How do you count less than one beat? Here's a great way to count eighth notes. For a simple grouping of two eighth notes, count the eighth notes "one, and": "one" for the first eighth note and "and" for the second. Many musicians use this way of breaking down the beat.

Here is a good example to help you understand eighth notes. There's an old song that you may have chanted at school or at camp with friends. It goes "two, four, six, eight, who do we appreciate?" Do you remember that one? This simple chant will help you feel the difference between quarter notes and eighth notes. Look at the example written out (see **FIGURE 3-8**).

FIGURE 3-8　Camp Chant

TRACK 4

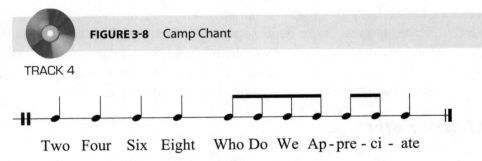

Two　Four　Six　Eight　Who Do　We　Ap - pre - ci - ate

Seeing the rhythms in a song will help you relate the concept of rhythm to something tangible. In **FIGURE 3.8**, you can really hear the eighth notes move twice as fast as the "two, four, six eight" lyric of quarter notes. When you practice this, use a metronome as a steady pulse. The first four notes should coincide with the metronome exactly. The last eighth notes should occur twice for every single metronome beat. That is because eighth notes are twice as fast as quarter notes. And that is exactly what your metronome is doing for you: providing instant, reliable quarter notes!

Sixteenth Notes

The beat can be broken down even smaller for the faster note values. The next rhythm is called the sixteenth note. A sixteenth note breaks the quarter note into four equal parts and the eighth note into two equal parts (**FIGURE 3-9**).

FIGURE 3-9   Sixteenth Note

Sixteenth Note = 1/4 of a Beat

As you can see, a second flag, or beam, is added to the stem to signify sixteenth notes. This is setting a pattern! Notes add more flags or beams to indicate faster pitches. You can also attach the flags of eighth notes to sixteenth notes and beam them together (see **FIGURE 3-10**).

FIGURE 3-10   Eighth and Sixteenth Note Beaming

TRACK 5

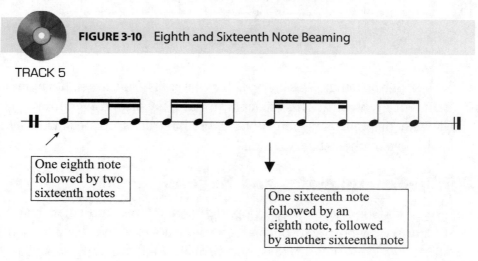

One eighth note followed by two sixteenth notes

One sixteenth note followed by an eighth note, followed by another sixteenth note

To help keep track of the sixteenth notes as they fly by, many musicians count sixteenth notes this way: "one, e, and, a." Since sixteenth notes tend to go quickly, "one, e, and, a" is something that you can say quickly. When you counted eighth notes, you used the pattern "one, and." With sixteenth notes you are using "one, e, and, a." Notice how both of these contain "one" and "and." That's because the notes are simply getting smaller and smaller, further dividing the beat. If you were to play eighth notes steadily on one instrument and sixteenth notes steadily on another instrument you'd notice that they both play on "one" and "and" together. The sixteenth notes simply squeeze another note in between those. That's a great way to see how the beat is divided. Look at **FIGURE 3-11** for some visual cues.

FIGURE 3-11   Eighth and Sixteenth Notes

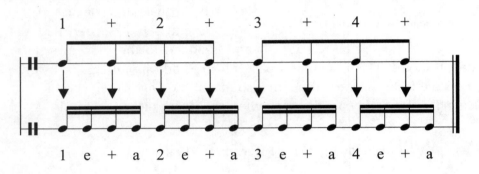

See how the notes line up across the staffs? The first eighth note coincides vertically with the first sixteenth note. The second eighth note coincides with the third sixteenth note. Everything lines up because rhythms are simple mathematical divisions.

Thirty-Second Notes and Beyond

It's possible to keep chopping up our beat into smaller and smaller parts. The next step beyond sixteenth notes is the thirty-second note. A thirty-second note breaks one beat into eight equal parts. Just like the transition from eighth to sixteenth notes, going from sixteenth to thirty-second notes will add another flag or beam to our notes (**FIGURE 3-12**). You can attach thirty-second notes to eighth notes and sixteenth notes by attaching their beams (**FIGURE 3-13**).

FIGURE 3-12
Thirty-Second
Note

Thirty-Second Note = 1/8 of a Beat

FIGURE 3-13 Beaming Example

FIGURE 3-13   Beaming Example

Again, you can go faster than a thirty-second note by continually cutting the beat in half. Faster than a thirty-second note is a sixty-fourth note, followed by a hundred-and-twenty-eighth note. You get the idea.

Everything Else

You have learned now about most of the major rhythms that you will encounter in music. Sit back and pat yourself on the back. You took a lot in! Let's come just a bit further to complete your understanding of rhythms.

Grace Notes

A grace note is a one that is played right before a beat. These notes are quick notes stuck in before the main beat. A grace note is displayed as a miniature note or notes that come before a regular rhythm (**FIGURE 3-14**). To perform a grace note, you simple play the grace note as a quick pick-up to the beat. Grace notes have an inexact rhythm—they are meant to be "squeezed" in before the next main beat.

FIGURE 3-14   Grace Notes

TRACK 6

Ties

So far, our longest held note is a whole note, which receives four beats. What if you want to hold a note longer than four beats? The tie is the answer. Simply, a tie is a curved line that connects two or more notes of the same pitch and adds their rhythms together. By tying notes together, you can hold a note as long as you need by tying many notes together: This increases the length of the note to the sum of all the notes combined. You can actually tie from note to note, creating very long notes. **FIGURE 3-15** shows an example of a long tie using multiple notes tied together for a very long note.

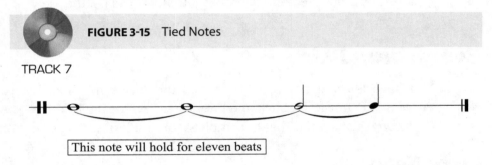

FIGURE 3-15 Tied Notes

TRACK 7

This note will hold for eleven beats

Remember, in order for notes to be tied, they must be the same pitch. When you play a tied note, you simply hold the first note for the total value. Even though there are many notes in a row all tied together, you simply play one long continuous note without repeating.

Dots

Placing a small dot directly to the right of any note increases the duration of that note by one half. For example, placing a dot after a half note makes the dotted half last for three beats. The original half note receives two beats and the dot adds half the value of the original note (a half note): The dot adds one extra beat (a quarter note), bringing the total up to three beats. Any note can be dotted. **FIGURE 3-16** is a chart of dotted rhythms and their duration.

FIGURE 3-16
Dotted Rhythms

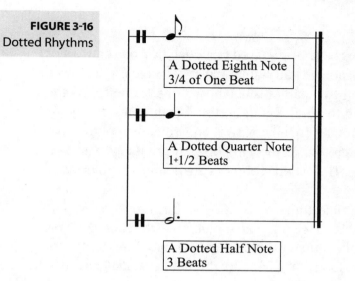

A Dotted Eighth Note
3/4 of One Beat

A Dotted Quarter Note
1+1/2 Beats

A Dotted Half Note
3 Beats

A dot extends the value of a note. A tie also extends notes. It's often convenient to show dotted rhythms as tied notes instead of dots. They represent the same thing—the notes last for the same period of time. It will be helpful for you to see what a dotted note looks like as a tie, as you may encounter either one (see **FIGURE 3-17**).

FIGURE 3-17 Dotted Rhythms as Tied Notes

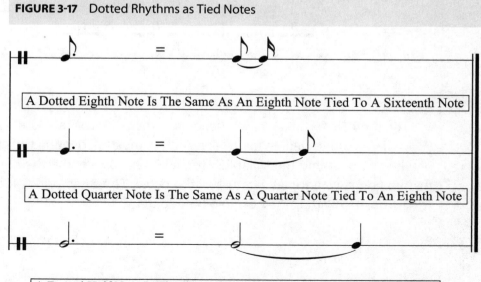

A Dotted Eighth Note Is The Same As An Eighth Note Tied To A Sixteenth Note

A Dotted Quarter Note Is The Same As A Quarter Note Tied To An Eighth Note

A Dotted Half Note Is The Same As A Half Note Tied To A Quarter Note

Triplets

Up to this point, rhythms have been based on equal divisions of two. For example, breaking a whole note in half results in two half notes. In the same way, dividing a half note in two parts results in two quarter notes. As the divisions get smaller, going through eighth and sixteenth notes, the notes are continuously broken in half, equally by two. The other side of the coin is to break beats into other groupings, most importantly groupings based on odd numbers such as three. These odd groupings are commonly referred to as tuplets.

When we break a beat into three parts, we give birth to a triplet. The most basic triplet to look at is the eighth note triplet. An eighth note triplet is simply three eighth notes that equally divide one beat into three parts (see **FIGURE 3-18**). You could also look at it as a ratio: three notes equally divided in the same space as one beat. Since there are three notes in each beat, eighth note triplets are faster than two eighth notes taking up the same beat. The more notes per beat, the faster they progress.

 FIGURE 3.18   Eighth Note Triplets

TRACK 8

The three notes are always beamed together with a small number three above the beam to denote the triplet. A great trick to counting triplets is to break each beat into the syllables "trip-a-let" as you say the rhythms. Any rhythm can have a triplet, not just eighth notes. The same principles apply when you are dividing the beat into other parts.

Swing Rhythm

Swing rhythm is a type of rhythmic phrasing that is most commonly associated with jazz music. It's very hard to describe "swing" on paper; it's often felt and heard by those who listen to or play jazz. Swing rhythm specifically applies only to eighth notes. Instead of being played as eighth notes evenly spaced as half of a beat each, swing eighths are phrased very differently. The first eighth note has a longer duration, about 65 percent of the beat, and the second eighth note compensates for this by being shorter. The effect is a lopsided eighth note pattern that "swings."

On paper, nothing looks different. All the eighth notes are written the exact same way. Swing rhythm only applies to eighth notes. All other rhythms are played normally. But you will see this symbol: ♫ = ♫. When you see that symbol, always above the first measure, it instructs you to play the written eighth notes as swung eighths. The symbol itself is an eighth note triplet with the first two eighths tied together. That's as close as musicians come to quantifying swing rhythm on paper. If in doubt, buy some Duke Ellington recordings and listen.

Chapter 4

The Long and Short of Rests

All this talk about notes and rhythms wouldn't be complete without some discussion about rests. The best news of the day is that everything you've learned in the previous chapters about rhythms also applies to rests. The only difference is that a rest tells you to not do anything! At last, we get a break.

Silent Notes

Every pitch needs duration. Rhythm defines how long notes should be sustained. Music isn't always about sound—rests are as common as pitches. Rests indicate a spot in the music where you don't play a sound. Since a rest does not have a pitch associated with it, it requires a different symbol.

For many students, rests can be a difficult and confusing element of reading music. It's easy to "do" something—e.g., play or hold out notes. Some find the absence of activity difficult. But if you can count a quarter note, you can count a quarter rest—they are the same thing; both receive one count. The goal here is to lay out all the symbols and group them with their pitched counterparts so you become familiar with them. You'll be a rest expert in no time.

Whole, Half, and Quarter Rests

The first rests you'll learn have the same duration as the first notes you learned about in Chapter 3. A rest can be the same duration as any note.

Whole Rests

You already know that a whole note receives four counts. A whole rest, which looks like this: ▬, is a rest that lasts for four counts. Whole rests always hang from the fourth line. Interestingly, they always appear in the dead center of any measure. This makes them very easy to spot. **FIGURE 4-1** shows a line of music that uses whole notes and whole rests. Remember to count carefully through each measure and use a metronome to help you keep accurate time.

FIGURE 4-1 Whole Notes and Whole Rests

TRACK 9

Half Rests

Dividing our whole rest in half brings us to the half rest. As you remember, the half note receives two counts. The half rest, which looks like this: ▬ , also receives two counts. You may be thinking to yourself, "Hey, that looks an awful lot like a whole rest!" And you're right. They look very similar. However, if you look closely you'll notice that the half rest sits on the third line, while the whole rest hangs from the fourth line (the line above it). The half rest looks like a little top hat. Have no fear! You're likely to never confuse them. Here's why: The next chapter explains meter and time signatures in depth, but for now, be aware that the most common measure has four beats in it—it's called common time, or $\frac{4}{4}$. Since the whole rest takes up four beats, you'll only see a whole rest sitting alone in a measure. On the other hand, since a half rest only receives two beats, you'll see it accompanied by other notes or rests in the same measure. Because of this, it's hard to confuse them even when you look at them quickly. **FIGURE 4-2** shows an example of half notes and half rests. Once you get the hang of seeing the whole rest and the half rest, you won't find it difficult to tell them apart.

FIGURE 4-2 Half Notes and Half Rests

TRACK 10

Quarter Rests

A quarter rest receives one count. Quarter rests are extremely common, especially in many of the easier pieces that students new to reading music will tackle. While the whole and half rest symbols may have confused you because they are so similar, the quarter rest promises to ease your pain. The quarter rest looks like this: 𝄽. **FIGURE 4-3** is an example with quarter notes and quarter rests.

FIGURE 4-3 Quarter Notes and Quarter Rests

TRACK 11

As always, count slowly and use a metronome. Learning to count whole, half, and quarter rests will equip you with the basic vocabulary of rhythms. **FIGURE 4-4** shows a whole smattering of examples combining whole, half, and quarter rests/rhythms. For the pitched notes, these examples use a single middle line B. This will let you practice without an instrument around— simply tapping with a pencil will suffice.

FIGURE 4-4 Quarter, Half, and Whole Rest Practice

TRACK 12

Smaller Rests

As you learned in Chapter 4, the smaller notes are denoted using flags on the stems, making it easy to spot and understand the smaller note divisions. Just like the pitched rhythms, the smaller divisions of rests use a system of flags.

Eighth Rest

An eighth rest, which looks like this: , is a rest for half of a beat. An eighth rest is a rather small rest with a single flag facing to the left (see **FIGURE 4-5**).

TRACK 13

FIGURE 4-5 Eighth Notes and Eighth Rests

Sixteenth Rests

An eighth note has one flag from its stem and an eighth rest has one flag attached to a small stem. So it would seem logical that since a sixteenth note has two flags, the sixteenth rest would have two flags as well . . . and it does! Here is the symbol for a sixteenth rest: 𝄿 . A sixteenth rest lasts for a quarter of a beat (see **FIGURE 4-6**). This is a very short time and will go by fairly quickly.

FIGURE 4-6 Sixteenth Notes and Sixteenth Rests

TRACK 14

One of the principal differences between normal rhythms and rests is that normal rhythms, more specifically eighth and sixteenth note rhythms, typically join their flags when grouped together. Very rarely do you see single eighth notes like this: ♪ ♪. More commonly, you'll see eighth notes joining their stems together like this: ♫. But eighth and sixteenth rests never join together. You will only see them as single rests.

Other Kinds of Rests

In addition to the common rests, a few more rests exist that you should know about to complete your understanding of how rests and rhythms work together.

Rests in Triplets

In the last chapter, you learned about a common triplet: the eighth note triplet. An eighth note triplet squeezed three equally spaced eighth notes into one beat. Inside of this triplet, a rest can be placed on any one of the eighth notes, resulting in three common types of rests inside of triplets. The rest can be on the first, second, or third eighth note of the triplet. You count these rhythms the same way when you play them and when you rest them: tri—pa—let for each of the three beats (see **FIGURE 4-7**).

 FIGURE 4-7   Eighth Rests Inside of Eighth Note Triplet

TRACK 15

You can vary a triplet in many ways; you can make any of the eighth notes into two sixteenth notes, and so on. The possibilities are endless. The most typical thing you'll see is the occasional rest inside of a triplet.

Dotted Rests

If you can dot a note, can you dot a rest? Of course you can! However, dotted rests don't occur as often as you might think. Let's use the example of a three-beat rest. You need to rest for three beats. If you wanted to play three beats, you'd use a dotted half note. While this may be common when dealing with pitched notes, you're rarely going to see a dotted rest. Instead, you'll probably run across a single half rest followed by a quarter rest. Honestly, it's usually easier to read rests written this way than to use dots. Most musicians like to see the beats of any measure laid out in a clear way.

With dotted rests, the same rules apply as with dotted notes: A dot adds half the value of the note it is attached to. In the case of the dotted quarter rest, which is common in certain meters, the rest would last for a beat and a half.

Chapter 5
Meter and Time

Music is held together by a sense of time and rhythm that is present in all music, regardless of genre. While rhythms and rhythmic notation define the length of the individual notes, meter and time signatures set up the bars and beats. But they also do much more than this. They set up the entire melodic and musical flow of music. Meter and time are the glue that holds music together.

Basic Time

Time and meter help to organize music. Rhythms convey only one small part of the larger picture. Time is indicated by what's called a time signature. A time signature follows right after the clef at the beginning of the piece. To many, a time signature looks like a fraction; while they have roots in mathematics, time signatures have their own logic and order.

In Chapter 2 you got a very rudimentary description of what a measure is. It went like this: A measure or bar is a way to group notes together. That was a true statement: that's what a measure does. However, the way in which it groups notes and rhythms together is dictated by the time signature.

Time Signatures

Time signatures indicate how many beats occur in each measure. It also identifies exactly which note receives the beat. A time signature is two numbers placed one on top of the other (see **FIGURE 5-1**). The top number always tells you how many beats are going to be in each measure. The top number can be any number except zero. While there is no limit to how many beats each bar has, you'll usually see numbers in the range of 2 to 12.

FIGURE 5-1   Common Time Signatures

$$\frac{4}{4} \qquad \frac{3}{4} \qquad \frac{2}{4} \qquad \frac{6}{8} \qquad \frac{9}{8}$$

The bottom number of a time signature tells you what kind of rhythm gets the beat. The last chapter would have you believe that a quarter note gets one beat. While that is often true, a beat is an open idea and any note can have the beat. As you can see from these examples, different numbers can take the beat. Very commonly the quarter note has the beat—but not always.

Unlike the top half of the time signature, which simply establishes how many beats are in each bar and thus can be any number, the bottom number of the time signature, which sets what note value receives the beat, can not be just any number. Table 5-1 shows the possible values for the bottom of a time signature and what notes they correspond to.

Table 5-1: Bottom Time Signature Values	
1	Whole note receives the beat
2	Half note receives the beat
4	Quarter note receives the beat
8	Eighth note receives the beat
16	Sixteenth note receives the beat

When you are confronted with $\frac{4}{4}$ time, which breaks down to four beats per measure and the quarter note gets the beat, does that mean that every bar of $\frac{4}{4}$ must have four quarter notes in it? No. $\frac{4}{4}$ time means that each measure must contain four full beats. This can be accomplished in many different ways. **FIGURE 5-2** shows examples of different measures of music, all written in $\frac{4}{4}$.

FIGURE 5-2 Examples of $\frac{4}{4}$ Time

Regardless of what time signature your song is in, each measure will contain the same number of beats in the end, but will do so with different combinations of rhythms.

Common Time

If you are just starting out reading music, you're going to encounter $\frac{4}{4}$. time often. For starters, it's a simple meter to understand and it breaks the beats up evenly and logically. $\frac{4}{4}$ time is a great introduction to meter and counting. In music history, $\frac{4}{4}$ time has been used so much that it has become "commonplace" in music. It's so common that $\frac{4}{4}$ time is often shown with a **C** in place of the traditional $\frac{4}{4}$ fractional time signature. The **C** symbol stands for common time, which means the same as $\frac{4}{4}$ (see **FIGURE 5-3**).

FIGURE 5-3 Common Time

That Explains It!

Back in the chapter on rhythms, when the notes and their durations were explained, many of you might have been confused. Why is a quarter note called a quarter note when it gets one beat? Quarter comes from ¼, so why doesn't it get one quarter of a beat?

You just learned about common time, which is the most frequently used time signature in music. It's also one of the oldest. The divisions of rhythms come more from the basic $\frac{4}{4}$ common time signatures than from anything else. Take a look at this list; it may clear up a few things for you.

In a measure of $\frac{4}{4}$:

- A quarter note takes up one quarter of a measure.
- A half note takes up half of a measure.
- A whole note takes up the whole measure.
- An eighth note takes up one eighth of a measure.

You can see that the majority of rhythms that we deal with take their name from divisions of a bar of $\frac{4}{4}$ time. Since a great deal of music is in $\frac{4}{4}$ time, counting is easy. You will see later that in compound meters the term beat changes quite a bit. What never changes are the relationships of the rhythms to each other. **FIGURE 5-4** may help to solidify the rhythms for you. Each row of this chart is equal to one bar of $\frac{4}{4}$ time.

FIGURE 5-4 Rhythmic Breakdown

Counting with the Time Signature

So far you've been counting the duration of notes and rhythms by counting how many beats they last. While this is an important and necessary skill, now that you know about time signatures, you should be aware of how time signatures help you count. Let's take a bar of $\frac{4}{4}$ for an example. In each measure, there are four main beats. If you had to play four quarter notes in each bar, until now you may have counted them as "one, one, one, one" because they each lasted for one beat. It's much simpler to think of each measure as having four counts. Each of the quarter notes takes up one of those counts. When you count the same measure, count it "one, two, three, four." Not only does this help you count all rhythms, it makes you aware of the measure and how many beats it contains. From now on when you count, you will count along with the duration of the particular measure. Let's learn about meter now and you can see this principle in action.

Simple Meter

A simple meter is any meter that breaks the beat up into even divisions. This means that whatever the beat is, whether it's $\frac{4}{4}$, $\frac{3}{4}$, or $\frac{2}{4}$, each beat (which is a quarter note) is equally divided. The beat is broken into even divisions of two (eighth notes), four (sixteenth notes) or eight (thirty-second) notes.

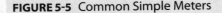

FIGURE 5-5 Common Simple Meters

What sets simple meters apart from other meters is how the beats are grouped together. The clearest way to see how beats are grouped is the use of eighth and sixteenth notes (see **FIGURE 5-5**). Since the flags join and are visually grouped together, you can clearly see how the notes and the beats break down. Whenever you see notes grouped together in twos or fours, you know that you are in simple time. Since $\frac{4}{4}$, $\frac{3}{4}$, and $\frac{2}{4}$ are the most common meters and all are in simple time, you will become a pro at simple meters in short order!

Compound Meter

Simple meters have one important feature: groupings of two or four notes. The next meters are compound meters. A compound meter breaks itself into groups of three. This is what makes compound time different from simple time. Common compound meters are $\frac{3}{8}$, $\frac{6}{8}$, $\frac{9}{8}$, and $\frac{12}{8}$. Compound meters usually have an 8 in the lower part of the meter because the meter is based on eighth notes receiving the beat.

As you can see in **FIGURE 5-6**, compound meters visually group sets of three notes. $\frac{3}{8}$ simply contains one grouping of three, $\frac{6}{8}$ two groupings of three, and so on. Counting in $\frac{4}{4}$ and other simple meters hasn't been such a big deal. You simply set your metronome or tap your foot along with the quarter notes. In a measure of $\frac{4}{4}$ you'd simply count as shown in **FIGURE 5-7**.

FIGURE 5-6 Common Compound Meters

FIGURE 5-7 Counting in $\frac{4}{4}$ Time

When it comes to compound time, you're probably not going to count each eighth note as it comes by. Your foot would get tired and you'd wear your metronome out! Instead of counting one two three four five six for each measure, we only pay attention to the groupings of three. By grouping the eighth notes in threes, players will place a natural accent on every group of three, making those notes jump out a touch. Because of the natural accent on the first of every three note grouping, we often count compound meters differently. Take a look at two measures of $\frac{6}{8}$ time to better illustrate this (see **FIGURE 5-8**).

FIGURE 5-8 Counting in $\frac{6}{8}$ Time

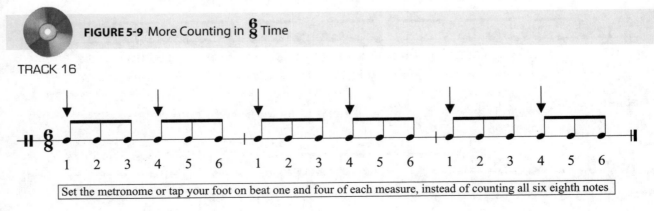

Musicians feel strong "pulses" every three eighth notes. In a measure of $\frac{6}{8}$ you'd feel two very strong pulses in each measure. Most musicians set their metronome or tap their foot to these pulses. This is a hard concept to read about; thankfully you have the CD to listen to. Listen to the meter examples and it will come to life very quickly for you (see **FIGURE 5-9**).

FIGURE 5-9 More Counting in $\frac{6}{8}$ Time

TRACK 16

Set the metronome or tap your foot on beat one and four of each measure, instead of counting all six eighth notes

Other Meters

In music, the combination of simple and compound time signatures will get you through the majority of the music you'll encounter. Even so, composers and musicians love to stretch the boundaries. All of the meters you've learned about so far have been divided into easy groupings. Other music exists in unusual groupings, called odd time.

Odd Time

Odd time and odd meter simply mean a meter that is asymmetric, or a meter that has uneven groupings. Odd time can be expressed any time that 5, 7, 10, 11, 13, and 15 are the top value in a time signature. The bottom of the signature can be any rhythmic value; it's the top number that determines if it's symmetric (simple) or asymmetric (odd) time. Let's start with a basic odd meter, $\frac{5}{4}$ (see **FIGURE 5-10**).

FIGURE 5-10 $\frac{5}{4}$ Odd Time

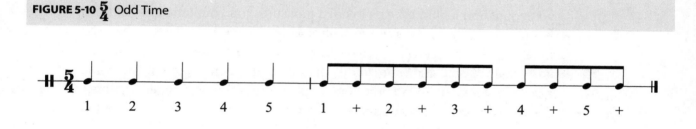

It would seem simple enough to count each measure with five beats and keep going. For many, this is not simple and takes some getting used to. There are a few reasons for this; for starters, most of the music you've heard in your life isn't in odd meter. When you move away from the symmetry of two- and three-beat patterns, it starts to feel unnatural and strange. With a little bit of practice you can get the hang of it. Odd meters require unusual rhythmic groupings. For example, look at a measure of $\frac{7}{8}$ and all the possible ways to group the eighth notes (see **FIGURE 5-11**).

FIGURE 5-11 Rhythmic Groupings in $\frac{7}{8}$

When rhythms are grouped together visually and beamed like this, it usually indicates to the player to phrase the music in the same groupings. To "phrase," the musician may place slight accents on the first note of each grouping.

Cut Time

Cut time is another name for $\frac{2}{2}$ meter. It can also be displayed as the symbol ¢. In $\frac{2}{2}$ meter there are two main beats in each bar. There appears to be four beats, as in $\frac{4}{4}$. So what's the difference? In a measure of $\frac{4}{4}$, you count and feel four beats in each measure: you count the quarter note. In cut time, you only count the half note, so you count twice per bar. Cut time is typically used in classical music at faster tempos. Since cut time is typically faster, there are more quarter and eighth notes. If the same example were written in $\frac{4}{4}$ you'd encounter more eighth and sixteenth notes. See the example in **FIGURES 5-12** and **5-13** for yourself; when cut time is opted over $\frac{4}{4}$ meter, it's typically easier to read.

FIGURE 5-12 Cut Time

FIGURE 5-13 Cut Time Written as $\frac{4}{4}$

Putting It All Together

Meter is a complex topic—the last few chapters have given you a good basic knowledge of meter, but there are still a few things you need to know about how meter is used and written in music.

FACT

Meters can change at any place in a piece of music. All that's required is a new time signature placed at the beginning of the measure. The new time signature applies until the end of the piece, unless you encounter another time signature that changes the meter again. Once a meter change is indicated, it sticks until it's changed again.

Multi-Measure Rests

A multi-measure rest is an easy way to count long stretches of rests. It appears as a long black bar with a number in the middle (see **FIGURE 5-14**). The number designates how many full measures to rest. This rest states that you are resting for eight measures in a row. How you count that rest is dependent on the time signature that the piece is in. The symbol for an eight-measure multi-rest will look the same no matter what meter you are in.

FIGURE 5-14 Multi-Measure Rests

$$\frac{4}{4} \qquad\qquad\qquad 8 \qquad\qquad\qquad$$

Pickup Measures

The length of a measure is dictated by the time signature. A measure of $\frac{4}{4}$ time must contain four beats in order to be considered a "complete" measure, right? Yes, in most cases. There is one exception. A piece of music can begin with an incomplete measure, called a pickup measure. The length of the pickup measure will vary; it really depends on the particular song or piece. **FIGURE 5-15** is a famous example.

FIGURE 5-15 Example of a Pickup Measure

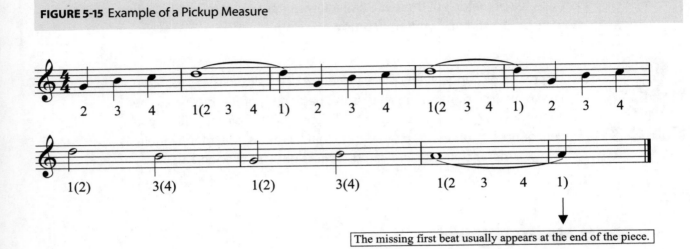

The missing first beat usually appears at the end of the piece.

This particular melody starts with a three-beat first measure. That's just how this melody panned out. The note "D" in the first full measure definitely feels like beat one. Because of this, the composer backtracked the first three notes into a pickup bar to let the rest of the melody sit where it's meant to. Pickup measures are very common in music. To count them properly, simply work backward from the first complete bar. If there is one quarter note in the pickup measure, the next measure has to start on beat one, so back up one beat and start counting on beat four.

Chapter 6
Conquering Rhythm

Rhythm is a far less tangible subject than pitch. A note is a note, simple as that. You can feel and hear notes. Notes have specific places on your instrument. Rhythms are less concrete. They are constantly changing due to tempo and meter changes. For many, rhythm is a major stumbling block and reading complicated rhythms is extremely difficult. Rhythm can be as concrete and easy as pitch if it's approached the right way. Rhythm can be conquered!

Overcoming Rhythm

Is rhythm really that hard? The answer to that question may lie in how you learned music. For the student who learned music in school, starting in third grade, rhythm most likely isn't a problem. It's not as hard for them because they learned it gradually over a period of time. The first few years might have been just quarter, half, and whole notes. While that student learned pitch, rhythm was reinforced, slowly building a foundation over the years. To that solid foundation of basic rhythms, more complicated elements could be added without much difficulty. By high school, this same student could read complex rhythms with little or no difficulty. This all happened over the span of eight to ten years.

But what if you didn't start reading in third grade? What if this book is your first experience in reading music? If you fall into this camp, you may soon discover that learning to read pitches isn't that hard. There is a concrete answer to "Where do I play that note?" When it comes to rhythm, most musicians who learn to read after they can already play an instrument have an extremely difficult time. Why is this? What makes it so hard?

First off, rhythm is a primal element. You don't have to think much about it. You can sing back a melody with the correct rhythm. You don't need to be aware of the meter or how to count in $\frac{4}{4}$, you just sing it and it's correct. When you read music, all of a sudden you have to count, keep track of the bar, divide the beat, etc. These all seem so unnatural, as all of your life you have simply "felt" rhythm and now it's becoming a mixture of math and science. It's no wonder that so many people have issues with rhythm! It doesn't have to be this way.

This chapter shows you how to simplify rhythm. Rather than counting each individual rhythm, you can learn to look for larger elements and groupings that will help you filter the music down to a manageable goal. If you sit down and think about how many different elements you encounter while reading music, your head may spin! Any element that you can simplify will make your job easier.

Common Rhythmic Divisions

There are some common rhythmic patterns that you see over and over again. Wouldn't it be great if when you saw any of those patterns you instantly knew what they sounded like? How much easier would that make your life? This is one of the secrets of great readers. While a good reader can divide any beat and count any rhythm, you'll find that the best readers have internalized rhythms and feel groupings and patterns naturally, without overly forced counting routines.

This chapter relies heavily on the accompanying audio CD. Please listen to these divisions and try to commit them to memory. The quicker you can do this, the easier time you'll have reading. Play these on your own instrument with any pitch you want, or simply tap them out with a pencil. Either way, focus solely on the rhythms, learning the patterns and internalizing them.

FIGURE 6-1 is an example in $\frac{4}{4}$ time that starts from whole notes and progresses down to sixteenth notes. As you listen to the CD, make sure to listen to the jump in note divisions. Each note is divided in half as the measures progress. Listen carefully to the metronome and how it keeps the steady quarter note beat regardless of what note division is played. Since the quarter note often receives the beat in music, learning how it's typically divided is vital. There are only a few ways to divide up the quarter note. Read about them and memorize how they sound, and you'll have an easier time reading them in the future.

FIGURE 6-1 Dividing Rhythm in Half

TRACK 17

Two Eighth Notes

This is a simple one. Divide the quarter note into two equal parts (see **FIGURE 6-2**). You can count it as "one, and" as mentioned earlier. The other way is to just listen to the rhythm and feel the division of the main pulse. The main pulse is coming from your metronome or your foot.

FIGURE 6-2 Eighth, Eighth

TRACK 18

Four Sixteenths

You can divide up a single beat into four equal parts using four sixteenth notes (see **FIGURE 6-3**). You can break the pattern into syllables again, "one, e, and, a." Again, better to listen to them. Notice that throughout this chapter, the metronome is set at the same speed on the CD and will not budge. That's your only point of reference. Listen to this over and over until you internalize the sound of these four sixteenth notes.

FIGURE 6-3 Four Sixteenths

TRACK 19

Mixing Eighths and Sixteenths

It's also very common to group one eighth note and two sixteenth notes together to divide a single beat. There are three possible patterns that these divisions can take. The locations of each of the three notes are rearranged (see **FIGURES 6-4**, **6-5**, and **6-6**). The resulting three combinations make up the most common divisions of one beat.

FIGURE 6-4 Eighth, Sixteenth, Sixteenth

TRACK 20

FIGURE 6-5 Sixteenth, Sixteenth, Eighth

TRACK 21

FIGURE 6-6 Sixteenth, Eighth, Sixteenth

TRACK 22

Listen to each of these divisions and internalize them. Write out a few examples for yourself to practice. Better yet, get a percussion book and just focus on your rhythm work. Do this even if you don't play a percussion instrument.

Dotted Eighth, Sixteenth

One beat can also be divided by dotting an eighth note and grouping it with a sixteenth note. The eighth note receives half of a beat, usually. When dotted, it now adds an extra one-quarter beat, bringing its total to three-quarters of a beat. You can also think of the dotted eighth note as three sixteenth notes together. To complete the beat is a single sixteenth note. This division also adds up to one beat; because of this, the notes are beamed together (see **FIGURE 6-7**).

FIGURE 6-7 Dotted Eighth, Sixteenth

TRACK 23

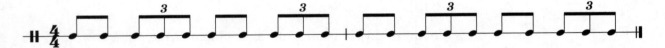

Transition from Eighth Notes to Triplets

Take two separate rhythms: eighth notes and eighth note triplets. By themselves they pose no great confusion or problem. However, when used together in the same bar, many readers get confused because an eighth note triplet is sort of like a very quick meter shift. Going from dividing in two to dividing in three takes some getting used to. The example in **FIGURE 6-8** shifts back and forth between two eighth notes and three eighth note triplets.

FIGURE 6-8 Eighths and Triplets

TRACK 24

Now that you've spent a little time with the individual rhythmic groupings, let's look at a nice long example that combines everything we've done so far (see **FIGURE 6-9**). It includes the common groupings, the rests and everything else! Try to see the groupings before you play them and relate them to the sounds in your head. Count along, but don't dwell on it. With a little practice, this won't be hard at all.

FIGURE 6-9 Reading Practice

TRACK 25

Hopefully, now when you look at music, you'll start to see the patterns and groupings that are common in music and better understand how to deal with them. You'll be able to sit back and just read music like you read this book—no more sounding out the letters and syllables. You simply look at the larger groupings of sentences and paragraphs. The same thing will happen with music as you progress.

Subdividing

Being able to understand basic rhythms and rhythmic groupings purely by sight is one way to accelerate your reading ability. You will continue to count rhythms; subdividing will simply make it easier. Some rhythms are very complex and you may need some help getting through them. A great technique to use is called rhythmic subdivision. If you've ever counted a whole note by saying "one, two, three, four," then you have subdivided. You're not really thinking of a whole note as its own rhythm; you're relating its duration to smaller notes—in this case, every whole note lasts for four quarter notes. Thinking like this is essential to learning rhythm.

When the music becomes more complicated, subdivision becomes more and more necessary. As soon as music utilizes smaller durations such as eighth notes and sixteenth notes, it makes sense to count the smaller note values. The reason for this is best illustrated by looking at **FIGURE 6-10**.

FIGURE 6-10 A Reason to Use Subdivision

In this partita by J.S. Bach, most of the piece is based on sixteenth notes. The rhythms are so prevalent that your mind starts to feel the sixteenth note as a common moving beat. Elements such as quarter notes and half notes feel very long after playing so many sixteenth notes in a row. In situations like these, it helps to think of the quarter notes as four sixteenth notes. It is easy to get conditioned to thinking of certain notes as long and certain notes as short. This is simply not true. Tempo changes throw all expectations of note duration out the window.

Subdividing means breaking beats up into smaller parts to count. Eighth notes are the first subdivision. As soon as you see eighth notes in your music, start subdividing the beat. Basically, you want to start counting the fastest notes that go by, which in this case are eighth notes.

Counting the faster note values will help you keep track of where you are. This means that you will count quarter notes differently. Instead of counting them as one beat, you'll feel them as two eighth notes together. The syllables "one, and" will come into play now. Each beat will be counted as "one, and" regardless of whether or not there are eighth notes there. The metronome will still click the quarter notes; you'll just count twice as fast. Look at the example in **FIGURE 6-11**.

FIGURE 6.11 Subdividing Eighth Notes

TRACK 26

The same will hold true for sixteenth notes and faster values. When the going gets tough, especially with complicated rests and ties, subdividing is the way to go. Simply count the fastest note value in the music. Doing so will help you keep track of all the rhythms and divisions.

Rests and Syncopations

We've largely ignored rests thus far. If you've studied up to this point you know that a rest is the same as any other rhythm, except there is no pitch associated with it. Since counting a rest is the exact same thing as counting any other rhythm, there is no reason to discuss it separately. However, rests have a great impact on music if they start to mess with your basic concept of strong vs. weak beats. This all leads us to syncopation, one of the more maligned concepts in music.

Strong Versus Weak Beat

Every bar of music has strong and weak beats. The strong beats always coincide with the meter and the basic pulses it sets up. For example, in a measure of $\frac{4}{4}$, there are four main strong beats. These beats coincide with the four quarter note pulses that are set up in a bar of $\frac{4}{4}$. Even if the bar is broken into eighth notes, the eighth notes that fall on beat one, two, three, and four are considered the strong parts of the beats (see **FIGURE 6-12**).

FIGURE 6-12 Strong Beats

TRACK 27

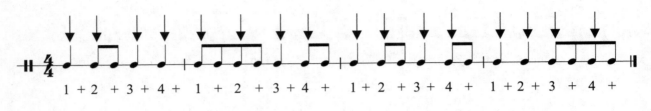

Arrows denote strong beats. Notice how strong beats are always numbered while the offbeats are always +

The weak beats are the rhythms that fall on the "off" beats. Every other eighth note, for example, is a weak beat. Removing the strong beats from music creates syncopations. This occurs when the music writer places rests on the strong beats and notes on the off beats; tying notes together can create the same effect.

Syncopations

Syncopation forces an accent on an unnatural place in a meter. Every meter has natural accents. Syncopation places accents on parts that aren't usually accented. For many people, syncopation is difficult to understand because those strong pulses are what define the meter. Jazz music shows one of the best examples of syncopation. Much of jazz rhythm is syncopated, and it's no surprise that those who play and read jazz are very used to syncopations. Some experienced sight-readers who have never read jazz syncopations have been known to have trouble with syncopation at first, as they aren't used to reading those types of rhythms.

To get started with syncopations, look at **FIGURE 6-13**. Suppose this bar of music, with a measure of $\frac{4}{4}$, started with eight eighth notes in the measure. But then one of the strong beats was taken away and replaced with a rest.

TRACK 28

FIGURE 6-13   Basic Syncopations

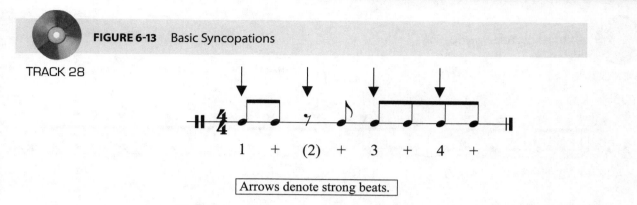

1   +   (2)   +   3   +   4   +

Arrows denote strong beats.

Now, imagine that rest placed on different beats until you are comfortable with the rhythms. When you are able to imagine music with none of the strong beats (**FIGURE 6-14**), you are getting closer to hearing syncopations. Here is the example without any strong beats.

FIGURE 6-14 More Basic Syncopations

TRACK 29

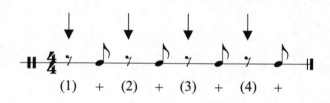

(1)   +   (2)   +   (3)   +   (4)   +

Arrows denote strong beats. All activity here is on the weak beats.

To play through these examples, the ability to subdivide is key. You should be counting "one, and, two, and, three, and, four, and" in each bar to help keep your place. This is especially necessary when you are syncopating.

Syncopation Illusions

In the last section you saw music with rests in place of the strong beats. Visually, this is a very clear way to present the information, as you can see the beats laid out nicely. However, not all syncopations are laid out this way—there are other ways syncopations can be written. **FIGURE 6-15** shows another common syncopation pattern using ties instead of rests.

FIGURE 6-15 Tied Syncopations

TRACK 30

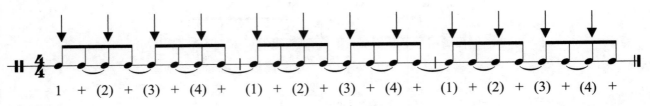

1 + (2) + (3) + (4) + (1) + (2) + (3) + (4) + (1) + (2) + (3) + (4) +

While rests stop sound and ties lengthen notes, the general effect is the same in that the ties cover up the rhythmic activity on the strong beats. Visually, this is much harder to deal with for the reader. Instead of ties, the example could be rewritten with quarter notes instead of the two eighth notes tied together (see **FIGURE 6-16**). (Remember that two eighth notes tied together equal the same duration as a quarter note.)

FIGURE 6-16 More Syncopations

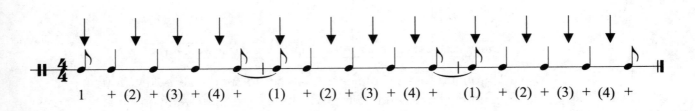

1 + (2) + (3) + (4) + (1) + (2) + (3) + (4) + (1) + (2) + (3) + (4) +

Arrows denote strong beats. These also coincide with the metronome pulse.
Notice how when the rhythms are written this way, it's very hard to see the strong beats.

Visually this is much harder to deal with, as the beats are very obscured. The counting below the bars shows you the subdivisions. Sometimes the greatest difficulty in syncopations is the notation itself and the clarity of the presented information. If you play a lot of jazz, especially big band music, you'll learn to read these groupings easily.

Practicing Common Rhythms

The aim of this chapter is to familiarize you with some of the common rhythms and groupings found in music. **FIGURES 6-17**, **6-18**, **6-19**, and **6-20** are some pieces to help you practice. These are rhythm-only pieces—you can play any pitch on your instrument that you choose, or simply tap on your desk. These will encompass anything and everything that has been covered in this chapter.

 FIGURE 6-17 Rhythm Etude #1

TRACK 31

FIGURE 6-18 Rhythm Etude #2

TRACK 32

FIGURE 6-19 Rhythm Etude #3

TRACK 33

FIGURE 6-20 Rhythm Etude #4

TRACK 34

If you are excited about rhythm, work on some more advanced rhythmic concepts that are beyond the scope of this book. Practicing rhythm as a separate concept away from the pitches is a great way to strengthen yourself as a reader and musician. Here are a few books on rhythm.

- Louis Bellson, *Modern Reading Text in 4/4*; Belwin Publications

- Ted Reed, *Progressive Steps to Syncopation for the Modern Drummer*; Alfred Publications

- Paul Hindemith, *Elementary Training for Musicians*; Schott and Co.

Chapter 7

The Language of Music

Music is more than just notes and rhythms. Opening up any piece of music reveals other symbols and markings that are crucial for making music. For the composer, these additional symbols convey exactly how the music should be played and organized. Elements such as tempo, dynamics, bar lines, and repeat symbols have their own specialized markings—and many of these are in another language!

What Language?

Italian is the most common written language of music. The majority of music uses standard Italian language symbols. Depending on the nationality of the composer, you may run into other languages. German composers sometimes write markings in German, French composers in French, and so on. If you run into these often, pick up a foreign language dictionary and look up every term in the music. Don't miss a vital clue because you didn't take the time to look up a word. Certain instruments deal with other languages more often than others. Classical guitarists, for instance, often play music of Spanish composers who mark up their music in Spanish.

In addition to this book, every student should have a pocket dictionary of musical terms. You'll find that the majority of the terms you run across in your studies are there—it's a great thing to stick in your instrument case.

Tempo

So far you have learned a lot about how to read the basic symbols of music: pitch and rhythm. Yet, at this point, your understanding of music is still basic, and many other symbols exist to reproduce flat two-dimensional symbols into rich three-dimensional music. Tempo markings are one such element.

Rhythm deals with the duration of pitches. The duration of those rhythms depends on the tempo of a piece. Tempo is defined as the speed of your musical beat. In the case of $\frac{4}{4}$ time, tempo governs how fast the quarter notes are. Tempo is a vital factor in music and is expressed a few ways: either numerically or in general Italian markings that have been in use for hundreds of years. Throughout this book, you've been reading that you should use a metronome to help keep your rhythm intact. It's time to learn more about how a metronome can help you.

Metronomes

A metronome is a simple device. The metronome, invented around 1815, has one simple job: to keep time without speeding up or slowing down. The first metronomes used a mechanical pendulum-type design that clicked from side to side. Metronome speeds are based on how many times they click per minute; this is also referred to as beats per minute, which are expressed numerically. All metronomes allow you to set their speed based on beats per minute, usually ranging from 40 beats per minute (a slow tempo) up to 200 beats per minute (a fast tempo). Beethoven was a staunch supporter of the metronome when it came out because it allowed the composer to signify exactly how fast a composition should be played. The metronome survives today because it is an effective tool for practicing music. Metronomes exist in two varieties: mechanical designs that you wind up and electrical designs that work on a battery.

Numerical Tempo Indications

Music written after 1815 may have numerical tempo indications that correspond to metronome markings. Composers give you the exact speed of the music and you set your metronome to that speed and play. Most modern music has metronome marks.

As you can see in **FIGURE 7-1**, the metronome marking is numerical and is shown with the note that receives the beat. In $\frac{2}{4}$, $\frac{3}{4}$, and $\frac{4}{4}$, typically the quarter note is counted, since the quarter note receives the beat in simple time. In $\frac{3}{8}$, $\frac{6}{8}$, $\frac{9}{8}$, and $\frac{12}{8}$, you set the metronome to count dotted quarter notes (every three eighth notes). As you learned in Chapter 5, compound meters are typically felt in groups of three notes. Instead of setting the metronome to count individual eighth notes, set the metronome to the dotted quarter (which is three eighths!). In the case of cut time, $\frac{2}{2}$, the metronome is typically set to the half note. In short, the metronome is set for the pulse of your song, which varies for each meter and each piece.

FIGURE 7-1 Metronome Marking

Expressive Tempo Indications

Before the age of metronomes, composers spoke of time and tempo in broad terms. Since most musical terms are rooted in Italian, tempo markings are Italian words that suggest a range of tempos (or tempi). This style of conveying tempo is the oldest and most standard way to show tempo markings. While you don't need to learn the entire Italian language, many of the markings you'll see will be in Italian, so it's worth knowing them.

No matter what form of tempo markings you are using, tempo markings appear at the beginning of a piece, above the first measure, usually just to the right of the clef. Tempo can be reindicated at any point in the piece if it should change.

Here is a chart of all of the common tempo markings and their corresponding metronome markings so you can set your metronome properly to practice. All of the tempo markings are approximate ranges of tempo. Musicians often have their own ideas of what these terms mean, which is why the terms are so general.

Tempo Marking	What It Means	Beats per Minute
Grave	very slow	40 BPM
Largo	slow	50 BPM
Larghetto	not as slow as Largo	55 BPM
Adagio	slow	60–70 BPM
Andante	moderately slow "walking tempo"	70–85 BPM
Moderato	moderate	85–100 BPM
Allegretto	not quite as fast as Allegro	100–115 BPM
Allegro	fast	120 BPM
Vivace	lively and fast	140 BPM
Presto	really fast	150–170 BPM
Prestissimo	really, really, really fast	170+ BPM

Another thing worth mentioning is that most metronomes have tempo markings written on them as a guide to help you. When in doubt, take a look; your metronome most likely has the markings and the approximate settings already printed on it, in case you forget. In addition to the standard tempo markings, there are a few words that modify the tempo to give a bit more direction. Here is a list of the standard terms you may encounter.

- a poco a poco (little by little)
- assai (very)
- molto (much)
- con (with)
- meno (less)
- non troppo (not too much)
- più (more)
- pochissimo (a very little)
- poco (a little, somewhat)
- quasi (almost like, sort of)

For example, if you see Allegro non troppo it means fast, but not too fast. Composers use these terms to suggest the speed and mood of a piece. Certainly, numerical tempo indications are the clearest of all, but composers still choose to use text to convey the general idea, allowing the individual performer some freedom to interpret. Listen to a few different versions of the same piece of classical music; you'll hear variation in the tempi of the pieces, among other things.

Ritardando, Accelerando, and Other Terms

So far, the tempo markings you've learned have related to the overall speed of any particular piece. But music is not a static thing and neither is tempo. There are times where you want to speed the music up a little and times when you want to slow it down a little. These instances don't need a full tempo change, especially when the changes are very subtle and short-lived.

Ritardando, which means "to slow," is used to denote sections that need to slow down gradually. This is useful at the end of a section when most melodies naturally feel like slowing down. But you can find a ritardando anywhere in music. Ritardando can also be abbreviated as rit. **FIGURE 7-2** shows a ritardando in action. As you can see, the ritardando is usually accompanied by a dashed line that extends under the note or notes that the composer wants you to slow down.

FIGURE 7-2 Ritardando

Accelerando is the opposite of ritardando: it means to speed up gradually. It is notated much the same way, with a dashed line extending under the sections. Accelerando is also often abbreviated as accel. **FIGURE 7-3** shows both rit. and accel. in action.

FIGURE 7-3 Ritardando and Accelerando

There are a few more common terms that apply to tempo and tempo changes that you should know. Many of these are similar to each other; still, certain composers opt for some terms over others.

- rubato (elastic tempo; speed up or slow down at will)
- ritenuto (slow down suddenly)
- rallentando (slow down gradually; abbreviated as rall.)
- più moso (a little faster)
- più lento (a little slower)
- a tempo (revert back to the piece's original tempo)

Dynamics

Dynamics, and their corresponding dynamic markings, are responsible for telling you how loud or soft to play throughout a piece of music. Dynamics are a vital element of music. Pay attention to them when you read music—they are as important as the notes and rhythms! Dynamics are an inexact science, since each instrument can produce varying degrees of loud and soft. Again, just as with tempo indications, Italian terms are used to communicate dynamics. Dynamic markings are always abbreviated.

Simple Dynamic Indications

In its simplest form, there are two basic dynamics: forte and piano. Forte, which means loud, is represented as a single *f*. Piano, which means to play soft, is always represented as a single *p* (see **FIGURE 7-4**).

FIGURE 7-4 Forte and Piano

FACT

Piano, isn't that an instrument? Pianos don't just play softly! The full name of a piano is a pianoforte because the instrument was capable of playing softly and loudly—something that other keyboard instruments, such as harpsichords, were not able to do.

If all you have is loud and soft playing, you won't be able to express a full dynamic range. There has to be some gray area and in-between dynamics. You can double and triple up on *p* and *f* to get extremely loud or extremely soft (see **FIGURE 7-5**).

FIGURE 7-5 Combined Dynamics

The Italian word mezzo, which means "in between," is a common word in music. When applied to dynamics, mezzo gives a few more dynamic options between piano and forte (see **FIGURE 7-6**).

FIGURE 7-6 In-Between Dynamics

Now that you know all these dynamics, let's look at the progression of dynamic markings from the softest to moderate to the loudest sounds possible (**FIGURE 7-7**).

FIGURE 7-7
Range of
Dynamics

ppp   *pp*   *p*   *mp*   *mf*   *f*   *ff*   *fff*

Soft ◄────────────────────────► Loud

Crescendo and Diminuendo

All of the text-based dynamic markings you have learned so far have imparted sudden and immediate shifts in the volume of the music you're playing. Two symbols exist to show gradual changes in dynamics.

A crescendo, which is a wedge shape that opens to the right 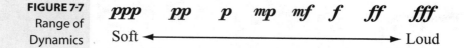 , instructs you to get louder. The length of the wedge corresponds to the length of the increase in volume. At the truncation of the wedge, there will be a new dynamic symbol telling you how loud you should be at the end of the crescendo. Crescendos (or crescendi) are most often seen as wedges, but you might also see the word written out or abbreviated as cresc. (see **FIGURE 7-8**).

FIGURE 7-8 Crescendo

A diminuendo is the opposite of a crescendo and is often called a decrescendo; they mean the exact same thing. Diminuendos (or diminuendi) instruct you to get softer via a wedge shape that is open on the left and gets smaller as it goes along ▭. Again, at the end of the diminuendo, you will see what dynamic marking you should be playing. The diminuendo can be written out or abbreviated as dim. or decres. (see **FIGURE 7-9**).

FIGURE 7-9 Diminuendo

Another modifier to dynamic markings is sforzando, which means "a sudden strong accent." If your dynamic moves to sforzando, which is abbreviated as *sf* or *sfz*, play a strong, sudden forte. You can also combine sforzando and piano dynamics together to make an *sfp*, which would mean to play a sudden strong forte followed by a piano dynamic.

Navigation in a Score

Music is typically read from left to right. However, there are symbols and markings that point out specific sections to repeat and play again. There is a navigation system that tells you exactly how to play a piece. The need for such a system lies in the fact that it's not easy to turn the page while you're playing music; most instruments require both hands to play.

Special Bar Lines

Bar lines do more than just break up the measures into easy-to-read segments; they also direct the player to stop or repeat the music. The first "special" bar line is the final bar line. A final bar line is necessary at the end of a section or at the end of the piece of music. It is simply a double bar line with a very dark outer line (see **FIGURE 7-10**).

FIGURE 7-10
Final Bar Line

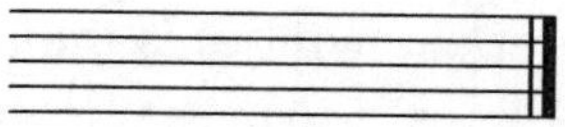

At the end of a section, a composer may place a double bar line to indicate some sort of change. You'll find double bar lines any time something in the music changes drastically (see **FIGURE 7-11**).

FIGURE 7-11
Double Bar Line

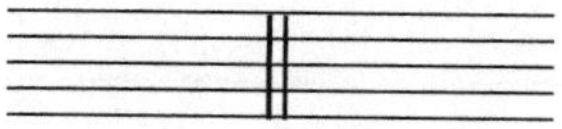

Repeats

The bar line can easily be transformed into a repeat marking. Repeat marks signify that a section, or even the whole piece, is repeated. Repeat bar lines come in two varieties: whole repeats and sectional repeats. A repeat symbol is simply a final bar line that has two dots. The simplest repeat sign is the whole repeat. A whole repeat will appear at the end of a piece of music. The dots face to the left (see **FIGURE 7-12**), signifying that you should play the entire piece of music again.

FIGURE 7-12 Whole Repeat

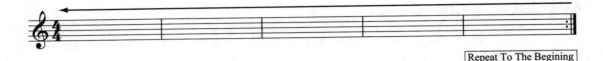

Repeat To The Begining

The arrow in **FIGURE 7-12** is there just to visually remind you where to repeat. In a real piece of music, you would only find the normal repeat markings, without the arrows.

The other variety of repeat symbol is the sectional repeat. A sectional repeat has two repeat bar lines, one at the beginning of the section and one at the end of the section. Whenever you see a repeat like this, you simply repeat the music between them. You'll notice in **FIGURE 7-13** that the repeat bar lines are the opposite of each other: the beginning repeat has its dots facing right, while the ending repeat has its dots facing left. This indicates which section should be repeated.

FIGURE 7-13 Sectional Repeats

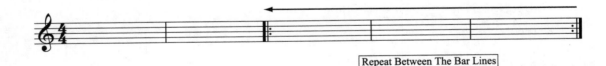

Repeat Between The Bar Lines

If a certain pattern of notes or chords is repeated exactly the same way, you may see a measure repeat symbol: ✕. This symbol tells you to repeat the previous measure. If the ✕ symbol sits on the bar line between two measures ✕✕, you are instructed to repeat the previous two measures. In long stretches where the music is identical, it's often less confusing to see these symbols instead of identical measures (see **FIGURE 7-14**).

FIGURE 7-14   Single and Double Measure Repeats

Multiple Endings

When traditional repeats don't fit into a particular situation, there are other options. One such option is the use of multiple endings. For example, suppose the music repeats a section of twelve measures and the composer wants you to play a different twelfth measure the second time you play it. Typically, a repeat sign works with exact sections only. For this example, the best option is to use multiple endings. In a multiple ending, traditional sectional repeat symbols are used; the only difference is that some measures are meant to be played the first time you play it and different measures the second time, most commonly called first and second endings (see **FIGURE 7-15**).

FIGURE 7-15 Multiple Endings

Play up to the repeat sign the first time through.
On the second pass, when you reach the "1" (first ending) you skip everything under that bracket and play the measures under the "2" (second ending).

The music under the section labeled "1" you play the first time. When you repeat, you skip all the music under the "1" and go directly to the section labeled "2." You don't play the first ending again because you already have. There can be more than two multiple endings, too! Theoretically there can be as many as the composer wishes, and the same rules apply. Keep repeating and playing the correct endings based on the number of times that you've repeated. Once you've finished the last repeat, you progress through the rest of the piece.

Codas

A coda, which comes from the Italian term for "tail," is a section at the end of the piece. A coda is signified with this symbol: $\oplus$. A coda is basically a transport symbol. When you come to a coda symbol, you magically jump from the symbol to the coda section, which has a corresponding coda symbol. This coda section is always at the end of the piece. The first coda symbol may have some other instructions along with it, such as "second time only." Traditionally, coda symbols are grouped with D.C. and D.S. symbols, which you're going to learn shortly. This will clear up what codas are and how they are used. So read on before you scratch your head in confusion.

D.C.

D.C., which is an abbreviation of da capo, literally means "to the head." The D.C. symbol is another way to signify that you should repeat a piece of music. When you come to a D.C. symbol, it means go back to the very beginning. It's often combined with other things, which are covered in the last section of this chapter.

D.S.

D.S., which is an abbreviation of dal segno, literally means "from the sign." D.S. markings always have an accompanying symbol, the sign or segno, which looks like this: ❅. When you see a D.S., you simply repeat back to wherever the segno symbol is. This is like a sectional repeat, just written out differently. Usually D.S. markings are combined with other things, covered later in the chapter.

Fine

Fine, which literally means "the end," is used to denote a place to stop. What's special about a fine is that it's typically combined with other symbols, such as D.S. and D.C. Fine is used in a situation where you need to repeat back to the beginning or other part of the music and then stop in a particular spot other than the last measure. The fine command is usually ignored the first time you see it; its significance only becomes clear as you read farther along in the piece.

Combining Symbols

Now let's combine the symbols. Coda, D.C., D.S., and fine are rarely seen alone. They are most often combined with each other to form instructions. **FIGURES 7-16, 7-17, 7-18,** and **7-19** are all the possible combinations of D.C., D.S., coda, and fine in real musical examples.

As you can see from the example, most of the symbols—such as fine, ⊕ and 𝄋—rely on information later in the piece to activate them. The first time you read through the music, you can typically ignore these types of symbols. As you progress to more and more complex music, you will encounter one of the preceding combinations that will bring those symbols to life.

FIGURE 7-16 D.C. al Coda

FIGURE 7-17 D.C. al Fine

D.C al Fine

Read the first two lines until the

D.C. al Fine.

Repeat back to the start of the piece

and end where it says Fine.

FIGURE 7-18 D.S. al Coda

D.S. al Coda

D.S al Coda

Read the first two lines until the

D.S. al Coda.

Repeat back to the 𝄋 and play until the ⊕

When you reach the ⊕

jump directly to the other ⊕ and finish.

FIGURE 7-19 D.S. al Fine

D.S al Fine

Read the first two lines until the

D.S. al Fine.

Repeat back to the 𝄋

and end where it says *fine*.

Chapter 8
Expression Markings and Other Music Symbols

As you advance to more difficult pieces of music, the music becomes more expressive. Playing the correct notes and the correct rhythms isn't enough. Composers strive to give exact information on how to play those notes. Through expression markings, composers can vary the attack and smoothness of certain notes. The rest of the common musical symbols help to clarify the thoughts and sounds of music.

Expression Markings

Without expression, music would be flat and boring. You could feed a computer a musical score and it would play a perfectly executed piece of music. The notes would be correct and the rhythms would be perfect. What's missing are the subtle nuances that only human performers give to music. Music lives and breathes; it's not a static thing. While many performers naturally bring their own form of expression to each note they play, there is a system of markings that give specific information about exactly what to play—and more importantly, how to play it.

Slurs

A slur is simply a way to connect two notes smoothly. Every instrument gives life to a slurred note in a particular way. No matter how your instrument produces sound, when you play a note there is an "attack" to each note. A slur is a marking that tells you to smoothly connect those notes and lessen the attack as much as possible. On a wind instrument, this could mean not breathing between each note. On a violin it would indicate to use one long bow. It's different on each instrument. No matter what instrument you play, a slur marking always looks the same. It is a curved line that connects two or more different notes (see **FIGURE 8-1**).

FIGURE 8-1 Slurs

TRACK 35

A slur looks suspiciously like a tie, and this is a common error. But actually, they are easy to tell apart (see **FIGURE 8-2**): A tie is a curved line that connects two of the exact same notes together. A slur is a curved line that connects different notes together. Here is an example for clarity.

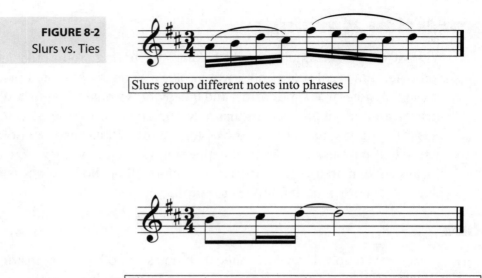

FIGURE 8-2
Slurs vs. Ties

Slurs group different notes into phrases

Ties connect the same note together to create an additive rhythm

In terms of notation, slurs are typically drawn on the alternate side of the stems. If the phrase had stems that faced up, the slur would be drawn under the notes; if the stems faced down, the slur would be drawn over them—this is simply to avoid clutter.

Legato

Legato is another Italian term used to express musical ideas. The word legato literally means "to unite or bind." Legato means a smooth connection from one note to the next. Legato and slurs may seem to be similar, but they are different. Legato is a way to phrase notes so that they are smoothly connected. Slurs are a technique. Legato will be written as a word above the section of music you are playing.

Phrase Markings

Sometimes slur markings are used to show musical phrases. Composers do this to show the larger sense of where the phrases are. Phrase markings look identical to slur markings; they just extend much longer (see **FIGURE 8-3**). It does not always mean that each note should be slurred—and in fact this may be impossible on your instrument. What it does mean is that you should do the best you can to connect those notes and make them sound flowing and well connected.

FIGURE 8-3 Phrase Marking

Articulations of Length

The length of a note is typically set by the rhythm. However, special articulations such as staccato and tenuto affect the overall length of notes with their own special symbols.

Staccato

Staccato is a marking that instructs you to play any note a bit shorter than it's written. Staccato is symbolized by a small dot that is placed directly over or under the notehead (see **FIGURE 8-4**). The staccato dot is placed on the alternate side of the stem. If the stem faces down, place the dot above the notehead; if the stem faces up, place the dot below it.

FIGURE 8-4 Staccato

TRACK 36

Staccato is an inexact science. There is no rule to tell you just how short the note should be; it just means to play it shorter than it's written. Staccato is typically reserved for faster note values—usually quarters, eighths, and sixteenths. It wouldn't make much sense to have a staccato whole note! A staccato is an effective way for a composer to space out notes without having to write faster note values and rests; it's easier for players to read staccatos.

Staccatissimo

Staccatissimo is the more extreme version of staccato. It indicates that the note should be played as short as humanly possible. Staccatissimo has its own symbol, shown in **FIGURE 8-5**.

FIGURE 8-5 Staccatissimo

Staccatissimos follow the same rules as staccato markings in terms of how and when they are placed. You will never see a staccatissimo marking on the longer notes.

Tenuto

A tenuto marking simply tells you to play a note for its full written value. A tenuto is a small flat line above or below the notehead (see **FIGURE 8-6**).

FIGURE 8-6 Tenuto

Tenuto markings are handy when you have a myriad of staccato markings and one or more notes needs to be obviously longer than the rest. Sometimes placing the tenuto marking on those notes draws attention to them, more so than just removing the staccato does. Besides holding a note out for its full value, a tenuto marking typically implies that the note should have a bit more weight to it than normal. In this case, tenuto markings have more than one meaning. Markings that affect the strength and loudness of notes deserve their own heading. So without further ado . . .

Articulations of Strength

Dynamics deal with larger sections of music and changes in the loudness or softness. When single notes, or selected notes, need to be played louder or softer, special symbols are used to denote changes in the strength and weight of those notes. These indicate to the player more information about how to play that note.

Accents

You have learned about dynamic markings such as forte and piano. Dynamic markings change the volume of sections of music. While it's possible to mark one single note loud and the next one soft with forte and piano indications, it's impractical to do so. The accent marking, which looks like this: > , is a way for certain notes to jump out a touch (see **FIGURE 8-7**). When you see accent markings, give those notes more stress and dynamic level than the other notes. The composer wants those notes to stand out of the music, so give them a bit more weight and energy.

FIGURE 8-7 Accent Markings

TRACK 37

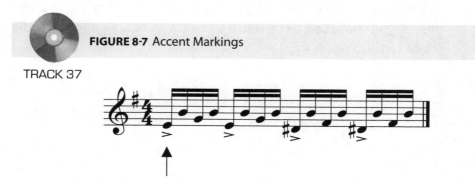

You'll see accent markings alternate of the stems—either above or below. This is consistent with the other markings you have seen in this chapter. Most extra markings go on the alternate side of the stems so they don't get in the way.

Marcato

A marcato is akin to a superaccent (see **FIGURE 8-8**). When you encounter marcato symbols, play those notes with great strength and great accent. Those notes should jump right out of the music. Following the trend of other musical symbols, marcato markings hover under or over the notes that they affect—always on the alternate side of the stem.

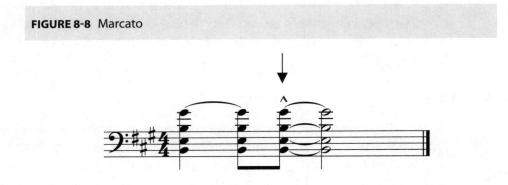

FIGURE 8-8 Marcato

Simile

If any of the articulations listed in this chapter go on for a prolonged period of time without break, it may be more efficient for the composer to write a bar or two of the articulations and simply say simile for the rest of the music (see **FIGURE 8-9**). The simile instructs you to continue the articulations until further notice.

FIGURE 8-9 Simile

At the point when you should stop playing those articulations, the composer manually writes out the last measure of the articulations. After that, if the composer wanted to remove those articulations, the bars would be written without them. Take a look at **FIGURE 8-10** to see how this is done.

FIGURE 8-10 Ending a Simile Passage

TRACK 38

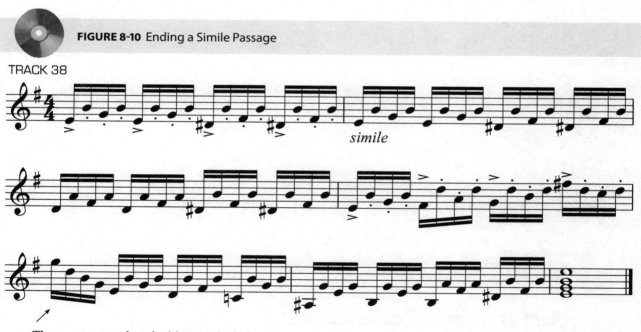

These notes are played without articulation

Combined Articulations

Articulations can be combined together; they need not be singular in purpose. You can have a staccato note with an accent. Almost any of the articulations can be combined together. **FIGURE 8-11** shows all the possible combinations of articulations.

The only articulations that can't be combined are ones that mean the same thing. For example, since staccato and staccatissimo mean the same thing to varying degrees, you'll never see them combined. Also, accents and marcatos wouldn't be combined for the very same reason. Everything else can and will be combined at the discretion of the composer and the music.

FIGURE 8-11 Combined Articulations

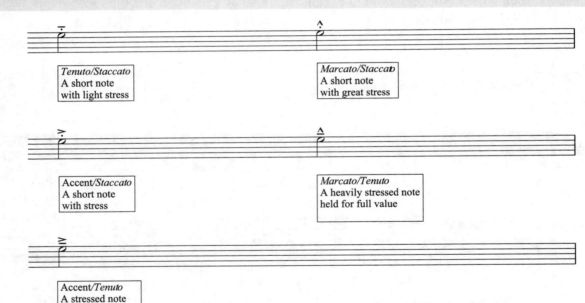

Performance Indications

The next batch of musical markings are grouped under performance indications because they give you information about how to play a piece— or, how not to play. These indications are different than expression markings. They are essential, common musical symbols you will encounter.

Breath Marks

When playing a wind instrument or singing, the element of breathing becomes an important part of musical flow. While it's a no-brainer that you have to breathe at some point, the point at which you breathe can define the phrases. Breathing can make or break a phrase! **FIGURE 8-12** shows what a breath mark looks like.

FIGURE 8-12 Breath Mark

Not only is the breath mark a common symbol to read, but it will also aid in your own practice if you play brass or woodwinds or sing; you can mark up your own phrases to assist in performing.

Caesura

Music doesn't always flow from measure to measure. Music is very much like water in that it ebbs and flows naturally. Music also takes pauses. One such pause is called the caesura. A caesura, which is signified as a 〰, allows music to suddenly take a brief pause. When you come across a caesura, you take a slight pause of an indeterminate length. You don't have time to get a sandwich! It's just a short point of rest. If you are playing with other players, such as in chamber groups, choirs, orchestras, or bands, caesuras need to be agreed upon. If you play with a conductor, she will usually cue everyone in together. When playing alone, you are in control of the length of a caesura.

Fermata

A fermata is the opposite of a caesura: A fermata extends the length of a note by an indeterminate amount. Fermatas can affect single notes or chords.

You typically find fermatas at the end of sections and at the conclusion of musical phrases (see **FIGURE 8-13**). Like caesuras, fermatas don't go on forever. The conductor, other players, or you will dictate their length.

FIGURE 8-13 Fermata

Octave Signs

Since the musical alphabet only gives players seven letters to work with, the same letter names are played in different "octaves" across the music staff. Sometimes when parts reach too high on the staff and excessive ledger lines are required, they can be very difficult to read. Music has a set of symbols that allow the notes to be written in a comfortable range while indicating to the player to manually adjust the notes up or down in octaves. These markings make the player's life easier. No one likes to read notes that are too high or too low.

If the composer wishes you to play one octave higher, the music will be marked with an *8va*, *8va*, or all'ottava, literally means "at the octave." An *8va* marking would appear above the notes that should be played up one octave. A dotted line extends out over all the notes that are to be raised up. The last note under the dotted line has either a small downward hook, or the word loco, which means "at place," or back to normal. Let's take a look at an example before (**FIGURE 8-14**) and after (**FIGURE 8-15**) an *8va* marking and you decide which you'd rather read. The *8va* symbol is typically only used on treble clef parts.

FIGURE 8-14 Without *8va*

FIGURE 8-15 With *8ᵛᵃ*

8ᵛᵇ, which stands for ottava bassa, is used when the composer wants a part played one octave down. The *8ᵛᵇ* sign is placed under the notes to lower them. You will only see this used on bass clefs. Its notation mirrors the *8ᵛᵃ* markings with a long outstretched dashed line extending across the affected notes (see **FIGURES 8-16** and **8-17**). The term loco is traditionally placed at the end of a section to remind the player to return to the normal notes as written. Again, look at the notation and decide which you'd rather read!

FIGURE 8-16 Before *8ᵛᵇ*

FIGURE 8-17 After *8ᵛᵇ*

While it's rare, it does happen that you have to raise or lower a section by two octaves. The piano is the best example of this due to its large range in either direction. Other instruments read these markings too! *15ma*, or quindicesima, translates to "at the fifteenth," which is two octaves up. The rules for its placement are the same as *8va*—the only difference is that you raise up to the second octave. Likewise, *15ma* bassa lowers a part two octaves. The same rules apply for placement as with *8vb*. These are rarely seen, but they do occur from time to time.

Miscellaneous Symbols

There are still a few symbols that you haven't learned about yet. The rest of the symbols are hard to group together in any other way than lumping them together as miscellaneous. Apart from the next chapter, which deals with instrument-specific notation, this is the last of the notation in this book! Whew!

Trills

Trills, which fall into the larger category of ornaments, are ways to dress up notes. This technique of ornamenting notes was very popular in the Baroque era. A trill is a rapid alternation of a note and the next note above it (see **FIGURE 8-18**).

FIGURE 8-18 Trills

TRACK 39

As you can see, a trill is represented either by a tr and/or the *tr* symbol. All that is shown is the principal note and the trill symbol above it. The duration of the principal note determines how long the trill lasts. You rapidly alternate between the principal note and the note immediately above it as many times as you can in the time allotted. In a traditional trill, you start with the upper note. If you see a C with a trill sign above it, the trill starts on the D above. In certain time periods, trills were reversed and began with the principal note, so you must be aware of when the music was written to know which is correct.

Trills have a few quirks that you need to know about. First, the upper note that you trill from is taken from the key or scale that the piece is currently in. From the original written pitch, you go up one note in the scale and alternate back and forth quickly. You can place a ♯ or a ♭ symbol either next to the trill symbol or above it to denote that the upper note is altered.

The most standard definition of a trill is to start the trill on the upper note. However, in the Romantic period, trills turned around and the figure started on the principal note and trilled upward. This is the opposite of how trills were performed before this period. There is no difference in the notation of either; you just have to know the age of the piece you are playing and what was stylistically correct when it was written to know what the composer intended. For most music, you trill starting with the upper note.

Ossia Measures

An ossia (meaning "or else") measure is a floating alternate measure that gives you an alternate phrase of music to play. The ossia measure will be written above the measure you are playing, or below a joined grand staff. Ossia measures are used to write out trills and other difficult ornaments (see **FIGURE 8-19**). They can also illustrate another way to play a selection of music. Simply, an ossia is an alternate measure of music that you can play instead of the normal measure.

FIGURE 8-19 Ossia

As you can see, the ossia measure seems to hang from nowhere above the measure in question. In this case, the ossia measure spells out how the trill is to be played. You find these often in Baroque music where many of the difficult ornaments need clarification. An ossia can also be used to provide an easier alternative for a difficult phrase.

Tremolo

A tremolo is a fast set of repeating notes. String players very often have to play long stretches of repeated notes. Instead of writing each one out, tremolo shorthand can be used (see **FIGURE 8-20**). But tremolo does not always mean the same note. If you are playing a piece where two or more notes are repeated for a long time, a tremolo marking can be used as well (see **FIGURE 8-21**).

FIGURE 8-20
Tremolo

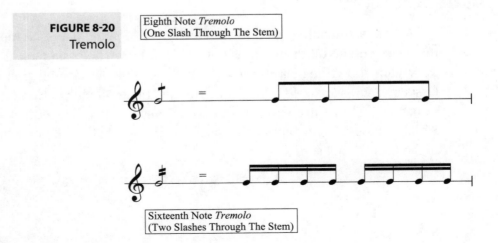

Eighth Note *Tremolo*
(One Slash Through The Stem)

Sixteenth Note *Tremolo*
(Two Slashes Through The Stem)

FIGURE 8-21
Interval Tremolo

The number of slanted stems between the notes signifies the rhythm of the repeated tremolo while the rhythmic duration of the principal notes signifies the length of the tremolo. It's much easier to see a half note with a tremolo sign through its stem than to see bar after bar of identical sixteenth notes—at sixteen notes per bar, it can be very easy to get lost. Tremolos are very common for string players and pianists. In theory, any instrument can have them.

Glissando

A glissando is something that most of us have performed on a piano. Have you ever walked up to a piano and dragged your finger across the white keys? That's a glissando. It's merely shorthand to signify that you rapidly slide through all those notes. A glissando is signified by a starting and ending note, with a long line connecting the two notes. The term gliss may or may not accompany the wavy line (see **FIGURE 8-22**).

FIGURE 8-22
Glissando

Piano and harp glissandi easily, as it simply requires dragging your hand across the instrument. Other instruments that perform glissandos do so "chromatically," as they play every note possible between the starting and ending point. It's most typically seen in piano and harp music.

Chapter 9

Instrument-Specific Notation

Each instrument conforms to the standard practice of music. No matter what instrument you play, you'll see notes, rhythms, and staffs. Particular instruments need specialized notation and symbols to accurately convey how to play them. This chapter will deal with common instruments and their own specific notation issues.

Strings

Strings—more specifically bass, cello, viola, and violin (guitar gets its own category later in this chapter)—have some notation symbols that are unique to strings and only strings. Here are the most significant ones you need to know.

Bowings

Stringed instruments produce sound by dragging a bow made of hair across the strings. Bows can either be pulled down or pushed up against the string. Bowings are a key part of string music reading and writing. Knowing how to bow a passage takes practice and experience. Even professional orchestral music contains some bowing markings to assist the players. There are two separate symbols for up bows and down bows (see **FIGURE 9-1**).

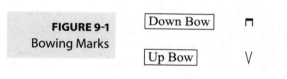

FIGURE 9-1
Bowing Marks

Down bows are generally stronger and more forceful than up bows. Down bows are typically used on notes that fall on the downbeats. Up bows are used typically on upbeats. But, of course, there are exceptions. Complex sections of music require complicated bowings in order to be properly executed. For a strings player, reading these symbols is as normal as reading the notes themselves. When you watch a professional symphony orchestra, watch how all of the bows move in the same direction!

ALERT!

Instrument-specific notation is a huge topic, one that could easily fill its own book. This chapter covers the basic notation for the largest groups of instruments. You will encounter the finer details while studying your own instrument's music.

Pizzicato and Arco

Stringed instruments don't necessarily have to play with the bow. A technique called pizzicato instructs the player to pluck the notes with his finger, instead of using the bow. The result is a short, staccato-like thump. It's a wonderful sound! Pizzicato is shown with a small pizz. above the note where the pizzicato begins.

Like many musical symbols, you only have to show the start of the pizzicato—it is implied that it goes until further notice. When the composer wants the player to return to regular bowed playing, a new symbol is needed: arco. At the end of a pizzicato section, an arco symbol instructs the player to return to regular bowing technique. **FIGURE 9-2** is a cello piece showing both pizzicato and arco makings.

FIGURE 9-2 Pizzicato and Arco

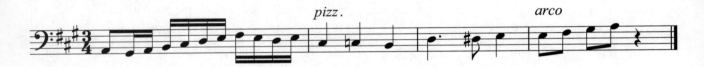

Other Bowing Techniques

Here is a list of special bowing techniques found in the string family:

- *spiccato:* The bow bounces off the string, producing a light staccato sound.
- *ricochet bowing:* The bow is dropped forcibly against the string, causing a loud stuttering sound as the bow ricochets across the string.
- *col legno:* The wooden side of the bow is used to tap the string. (A really cool sound!)
- *sul tasto:* Bow up over the fingerboard for a sweet, warm tone.
- *sul ponticello:* Bow as close to the bridge as possible to achieve a sharp, almost metal sound.

Slurs

On string instruments, slurs are treated differently than on other instruments. A slur is a smooth connection between two notes. On a stringed instrument, the smoothest way to connect two notes is to play them in the same bowing. This means that the player does not restrike each note; rather, she lets the bow pull through each note. The lack of attack gives the stringed instrument slur an extremely connected legato sound. Because a string player can fit many notes into one bowing, it's possible to have very long sections without any attack (see **FIGURE 9-3**).

FIGURE 9-3 String Slurs

Brass

The brass family—which encompasses the trumpet, French horn, trombone, baritone, euphonium, and tuba—has few specific notation issues compared to other instruments. One of the characteristics of the brass family requiring special notation is the use of mutes to change the color of the sound and the quality of the attack.

Mutes

One aspect that makes the brass family unique is its use of mutes. A mute is an object that is placed in the bell of the instrument to muffle and obscure the sound. The mute changes the tone and color of the instrument. Composers so often use mutes that brass players typically carry a mute bag with them to hold all the various mutes they need. The common types of mutes are:

- Straight mute
- Harmon mute
- Cup mute

Only the trumpet and trombone uses all three mutes; the other brass instruments just utilize straight mutes. In brass music when the composer wants players to use a mute, you'll simply see instructions as to which mute to use, when to start, and when to stop.

Slurs and Tonguing

On brass instruments, slurs are performed by not reattacking the note or notes. In the brass family, a technique called tonguing is used to separate pitches normally. Simply, the player uses her tongue to stop the air stream between notes and begin each attack. Since a slur calls for as smooth a connection as possible, the player simply connects the notes by blowing right through the passage, without tonguing.

Wind Instruments

With the exception of mutes, wind instruments follow almost exactly the same notation rules and exceptions that brass instruments do. Some of the individual instruments have some very specialized notation, such as flute flutter tonguing and such, but these are advanced topics too complex to cover here. As winds and brass all rely on the player to breathe the notes to life, many of the same techniques for slurs, legato, and tonguing apply.

Multiple Voices on One Staff

The last set of instruments that must be covered all have the capability to play more than one note at the same time. Piano and guitar are both able to play more than one pitch simultaneously. To further complicate this issue, these instruments are able to hold different notes for different lengths. Let's look at an example using the piano (see **FIGURE 9-4**). This fairly simple line shows a series of notes held in whole notes.

FIGURE 9-4 Piano Part One

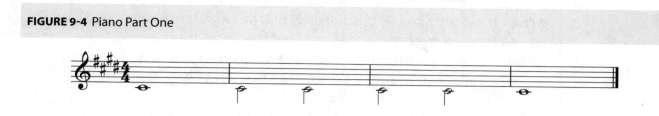

But the piano is capable of doing more than just playing one note at a time. **FIGURE 9-5** shows a line that you could play in addition to the first part. It's possible to play both parts at the same time. The low notes can easily be sustained while the pianist plays the upper voice.

FIGURE 9-5 Piano Part Two

But having to read two lines at once isn't practical. Instead they can be combined into one staff using "voices." A voice is a part of music that follows the basic musical rules. Each voice will have the correct number of beats per bar. If we combine these two parts together, we get the line shown in **FIGURE 9-6**.

FIGURE 9-6 Combined Piano Part

As you can see, each voice follows the rules of $\frac{4}{4}$ time for each measure. One of the main attributes of placing multiple voices in the same staff is to stem the voices opposite of each other. By placing the upper voice's stems upward and the lower voice's stems downward, it's easy to see what's going on. At first, seeing this notation may be a bit confusing, but it's necessary when instruments can not only play more than one note at a time, but can also hold them out to different lengths. Since piano reads in two clefs and is played with ten fingers, it's possible to have five voices in each staff! Talk about sight-reading!

No matter how many voices there are, the rhythms must vertically line up. Beat one will be at the leftmost part of the bar, regardless of what voice it's in. If two voices play beat one together, then the notes will be vertically aligned. Many players find music easier to read when it adheres to this system. This is because you can see the flow of notes from left to right so easily.

Rolled Chords

Any instrument that is capable of playing a chord is also capable of varying the exact timing of the chords. Traditionally, a chord is played with all the notes struck simultaneously. One way to alter this is to roll through the chord. Basically, a rolled chord is a technique in which you play all the notes in the chord in fast succession. Instead of striking the notes together, you "roll" through the chord. There is one symbol for a rolled chord and it exists in two variations: up rolls and down rolls. Since the player can roll the notes from either up or down the chord, both symbols are necessary.

As you can see in **FIGURE 9-7**, the rolled chord symbol is a wavy line with an arrowhead at either the top or the bottom. Depending on the direction of the arrow, roll the chord either up or down. If the wavy line has no arrowhead, it is assumed to roll up.

FIGURE 9-7
Rolled Chords

Roll Up   Roll Down

Braces

Any instrument that reads more than one staff at a time (most notably piano, harp, organ, and marimba) must have its staffs braced together to indicate that the lines of music are to be played together. A brace connects the treble and the bass clef to form the "grand staff" that you learned about earlier in the book (see **FIGURE 9-8**).

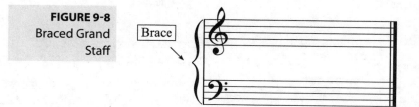

FIGURE 9-8
Braced Grand
Staff

Brace

Piano

Piano is one of the oldest and most popular instruments. The history of written piano music is long and distinguished. Amazingly, it has few special notational needs other than reading treble and bass clef simultaneously and pedaling.

Clefs, Voices, and Range

Because of the tremendous range of the piano, two clefs are needed to cover its range. Piano always reads in both treble and bass clef. Typically the right hand plays the treble clef parts and the left hand plays the bass clef parts—although this is not a steadfast rule. The upper staff can momentarily switch to bass clef while the lower staff can switch to treble clef at times. You will see a clef change in the appropriate spot and another clef change to return back to normal. Because the piano can play so many notes at a time, voices and multiple voices on the same staff are used. **FIGURE 9-9** shows a typical piece of piano music.

FIGURE 9-9 Piano Example

Also, because the piano has such an extreme range, octave markings such as *8ᵛᵃ* and *8ᵛᵃ* bassa are used to save the pianists from reading too many ledger lines.

Pedaling

The piano makes use of either two or three small pedals to change the sustain, dampening, and volume of the instrument. A concert grand piano has its pedals set up as shown in **FIGURE 9-10**.

FIGURE 9-10
Piano Pedals

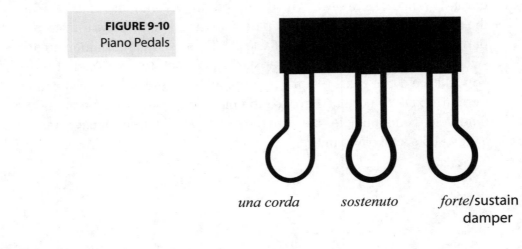

una corda   *sostenuto*   *forte*/sustain
                                  damper

Each pedal does something different. The pedals act as such:

- *Forte/sustain pedal, or "damper" pedal:* This pedal removes the dampers and lets the strings ring freely.
- *Sostenuto pedal:* When depressed, this pedal allows just certain selected notes to ring freely. This pedal is usually only found on grand pianos, not on the typical upright pianos found in homes and schools.
- *Una corda pedal:* This pedal shifts the piano hammers to the side so that they only strike one of the strings. A normal note on the piano is two or three strings played together. When this pedal is depressed, only one is played; the result is a softer sound. Una corda translates as "one string."

The damper/sustain pedal is the most commonly used pedal and has its own system of markings. When the damper/sustain pedal is depressed, a series of felt dampers are removed from the strings, allowing the piano's full range of strings to ring out. The symbols for depressing and releasing the sustain pedal come in two varieties: traditional pedal markings and modern pedal markings. Both do the same thing; you'll see both in music.

The sostenuto pedal is marked with a simple sos. and a bracket extending under the affected notes. Una corda is marked with u.c or una corda when the pedal is to be depressed and t.c or tre corda when you release the pedal. **FIGURE 9-11** shows how all of the pedals are marked.

FIGURE 9-11 Piano Pedal Markings

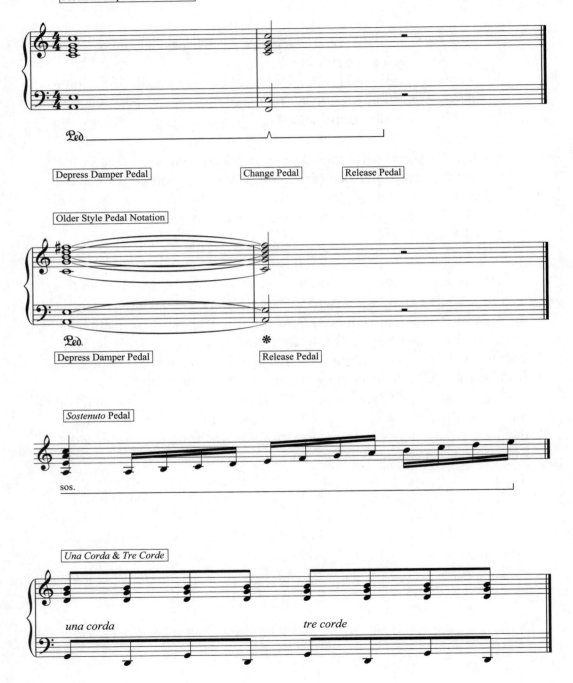

Guitar

Guitar is a complex instrument to notate. A myriad of unusual techniques, coupled with the fact that guitar can play the same written pitch in up to six different places, makes the guitar a challenging instrument to read and notate. It's really no wonder that so many guitarists have such difficulty reading.

FACT

This section is devoted to traditional guitar notation. Tablature isn't covered in depth here. If you're into guitar and reading guitar tab, check out *The Everything® Rock and Blues Guitar Book.*

The Need for More Information

The guitar needs specific notation. For example, top space E can be played in at least five if not six different locations on the neck. Signifying which location on the guitar can make the player's life much easier. It's for this very reason that guitar tablature is so popular—it tells you exactly where to play any note. Unfortunately, there is no rhythm with tablature, so it's largely ineffective. To combat this, composers can add some symbols to standard notation to better show where to play the notes on your guitar.

Positions

The guitar is broken up into "positions." A position is a four-fret area named by the location of your first finger. For example, the first position is when the player's first finger is on the first fret, second finger on the second fret, and so on. Guitar players typically play in positions because it's comfortable to do so. The guitar has about twelve positions. Electric guitars have more, but for most reading on the guitar, twelve will suffice. By signifying in what position a passage should be played, it removes the difficulty of wondering, "Which version of this note should I play?"

In guitar music, positions are signified either with Roman numerals that extend over the sections with dashed lines (see **FIGURE 9-12**), or traditional numbers. The Roman numerals instruct the player in this excerpt to play the melody notes in the ninth, fifth, and second positions. Without this aid, the player may not have reached this efficient fingering on his own.

FIGURE 9-12 Guitar Positions

Fingerings

In guitar music, specifying what fretting finger to use is an absolutely essential part of guitar notation. More so than with other instruments, guitar fingerings make or break a piece. This concern is so prevalent that you will find that the same piece exists in many different versions, all edited by different classical guitar players—all with different opinions on how to finger and play the piece. Fingerings will appear as plain numbers above or below the notes.

If a particular note is to be played on a particular string, the composer can indicate which string (one through six) by placing the number of the string in a small circle above or below the note (see **FIGURE 9-13**). By placing the string number in a circle, it's not confused with traditional numerical fingerings for the left hand.

FIGURE 9-13
String Numbers

Picking and Finger Style Notation

On the guitar, there are two ways to strike notes with the picking hand. Most electric guitar players use a small plastic pick to strike the notes. Like the other stringed instruments, the pick can strike up or down, much like a bow. Just like the other stringed instruments, the same symbols are used for up picking ∨ and down picking ⊓. Simple enough!

The other style of plucking notes involves using the right-hand fingers to pluck the notes. This is also commonly referred to as finger style. Classical guitar is always played finger style. In the classical guitar world, a standard system exists for naming the fingers that pluck the strings. They are as follows:

- P—Thumb
- I—Index finger
- M—Middle finger
- A—Ring finger

The names for the plucking fingers come from Spanish words. The PIMA symbols are written along with the other notation and, sometimes, the fretting fingers. That means that a traditional guitar piece may have traditional notation, position markings, string indications, right-hand fingering, and left-hand fingering. Guitar music has a lot of information to convey—just look at the example in **FIGURE 9-14**.

FIGURE 9-14 Guitar Example

Barres

Guitar players often employ a technique called barring. A barre involves lying the index finger down across the neck to depress more than one note with the single finger. Barring is a standard component of playing the guitar. In classical guitar music, barres are notated with specific markings to instruct the player when to use them. Barre markings correspond to the positions on the guitar. In addition to the Roman numerals, a small C is placed before the Roman numeral to denote a barre wherever the Roman numeral is depicted (see **FIGURE 9-15**). A barre at the tenth fret would read "CX."

FIGURE 9-15 Guitar Barre Chord Example

The only exception is the half barre, which is a barre that is applied to only the top three strings of the guitar. A half barre would have a ½ symbol before the C. So "½CX" would be a half barre at the tenth fret.

Pizzicato

Guitar can perform a pizzicato. If you think about it, guitar is always playing a traditional pizzicato. The standard string definition of a pizzicato is a note plucked with your finger instead of played with a bow—which is exactly what a guitar player always does. For the guitar to produce a pizzicato, the player needs to mute the string with his right palm and pluck the notes. The effect calls for a very short tone. The notation of pizzicato follows the same guidelines as it does in the section on string pizzicato in the beginning of this chapter.

Other Effects

The guitar is capable of producing a wide range of tone colors based on where the notes are plucked. Two terms are used in classical guitar writing to dictate exactly where to pluck the notes. Sul ponticello instructs the player to pluck at the bridge. The result is a sharp, metallic sound. Sul tasto is used to tell the player to pluck up near the fingerboard. The result is a sweet, mellow sound. By using these terms, which are borrowed from orchestral string writing, composers can show players how to play the guitar to produce a wide variety of tone colors.

Chapter 10

The Key to Music: Keys and Key Signatures

Music is organized with key signatures. Key signatures not only forecast the musical structure of a piece, they also help the musician read more efficiently. In addition to making you a better reader, understanding keys and key signatures will make you a better musician.

The Concept of Musical Keys

A key is the first level of organization that tonal music receives. Tonal music means music that uses keys, major and minor chords, and major and minor scales. Tonal music makes up the majority of music from the "common practice" period (circa 1600–1900) and is still very much in use today.

The concept of a musical key is very closely tied to scales, both major and minor. The simplest definition of a musical key is that a key determines the basic pitches for a piece of music. Keys are sort of the DNA of music more than anything else. A key is a slightly abstract concept, which can be a challenge to describe. A key defines what notes can be used to create an "expected" sound. As you progress as a music reader, keys and key signatures will become more important than just defining what notes to play. Keys can give you a glimpse into the mind of the composer and help you unravel how music is composed. In any event, you need to know a lot about keys and their key signatures if you want to be a good reader.

What Is a Key Signature?

Earlier in the book you learned about sharps and flats. As an alternative to writing sharps and flats throughout a piece, composers use a key signature (see **FIGURE 10-1**).

FIGURE 10-1
Key Signature

A key signature is used to indicate that certain notes are going to be sharped or flatted for the entire piece. It cleans up the written music for the reader and eliminates the need for overabundant sharps and flats that would otherwise appear throughout. A good reader will be used to reading in key signatures and prefer them.

Key signatures correspond to major and minor scales. Since a great deal of written music adheres to major and minor scales, key signatures are a convenient way to indicate keys and scales that are frequently used. Right now, we are talking about scales in broad terms. The next two chapters will deal with exactly what major and minor scales are, how they are created, and how they are used.

FACT

To musicians, scales are some of the most common elements of music. You can construct melody and chords with them. They are a pivotal part of understanding music and your instrument.

Chapters 11 and 12 will deal with major and minor scales in great detail. For now, you need to know the most basic definition of a scale. A scale is a grouping of notes that define a key. Scales are almost always made up of seven different notes. Each scale is different and there is a scale for each note in our musical alphabet (twenty-four). Another way to think of scales is that they are groups of sounds that can be used to create melodies and harmonies. Scales are a basic construction feature of music. Anyone who studies an instrument will have to deal with scales. Since composers write music using scales, knowing how scales work—and, more importantly, how to play them on your instrument—will give you a great advantage when it comes to reading music.

How Key Signatures Help Readers

Keys and key signatures help readers in a few ways. First, they clean up the music. The more sharps and flats that appear in the written music, the more elements the musician has to read. The more extraneous symbols you have to read, the easier it is to make a mistake. Since keys are regular and formulaic, key signatures are used often.

They also help readers by setting a regular pattern of notes for a piece. For example, if you read in certain keys more often than others, you get good at reading in those keys because you become familiar with those notes and what pitches are sharped or flatted. If you study scales on your instrument, key signatures won't pose a problem for you, as key signatures mirror the scales that the pieces are written in.

The System of Key Signatures

Key signatures use a specific system. Not just any note can appear in a key signature. There is an order and logic to key signatures that makes them understandable. Key signatures appear in two varieties: sharp key signatures and flat key signatures (excluding C major, which has no accidentals). A key signature will always display only sharps or only flats. You will never see both in the same key signature. Within the groupings of "sharp keys" or "flat keys" there is an order to how individual notes appear. Let's look at sharps and flats separately.

Sharps appear in key signatures in a specific order. Here is the order of sharps as they appear in key signatures:

F♯, C♯, G♯, D♯, A♯, E♯, B♯

The sharps always follow that order. Also important to note is that sharps appear in the same order. If the key has one sharp, it will be an F♯ . If the key has two sharps it will have F♯ and C♯. It always works through the pattern that way. A great way to remember the order of sharps is to use a little saying: Father Charles Goes Down And Ends Battle. The first letter of each word corresponds to the sharps as they appear. It's silly, but it just might help you remember.

Even though key signatures may appear confusing at first, most musicians would have a hard time reading without them. Constant flats and sharps placed throughout music can be more challenging to read than a single key signature.

Just like sharps, flats appear in a specific order. Just like sharps, flats will also appear in the same order every time. Here is the order of flats as they appear.

B♭, E♭, A♭, D♭, G♭, C♭, F♭

There is also an easy way to help you remember the order of flats: Just reverse the saying for sharps! Battle Ends And Down Goes Charles's Father. One saying gets you both sharps and flats—pretty convenient!

You know that if a key has one sharp, that sharp will be an F. But a staff has two Fs, so which F gets the sharp sign? Let's look at a fully loaded set of key signatures—seven sharps and seven flats (see **FIGURE 10-2**).

FIGURE 10-2 Correct Placement of Key Signatures

As you can see, there is a particular system at play here. When you have to write out key signatures, you can refer to the diagram here for clarity. All of the examples in this book have made regular use of varied key signatures, so you can glance through the book for reference.

Music may change keys at any time in a piece. The composer simply notes this by placing a new key signature at the point where the key change occurs. If you change from a sharp key to a flat key, you may get a "cautionary" key signature full of ♮s and then the new key signature. This is not standard practice, but it is found sometimes in written music. Otherwise, the signature will just change at the point when you see the new key.

The Circle of Keys

You'll find this handy "circle of keys" placed at the front of music books, music folders, and anywhere else music publishers can fit it. You have learned a lot about how key signatures work, and the way in which sharps and flats are placed in the keys, but you still haven't been able to define which key signature equates to which key. The circle of keys (**FIGURE 10-3**) is your first step in learning to identify the key a piece is written in, simply from looking at its key signature.

FIGURE 10-3 The Circle of Keys for Major

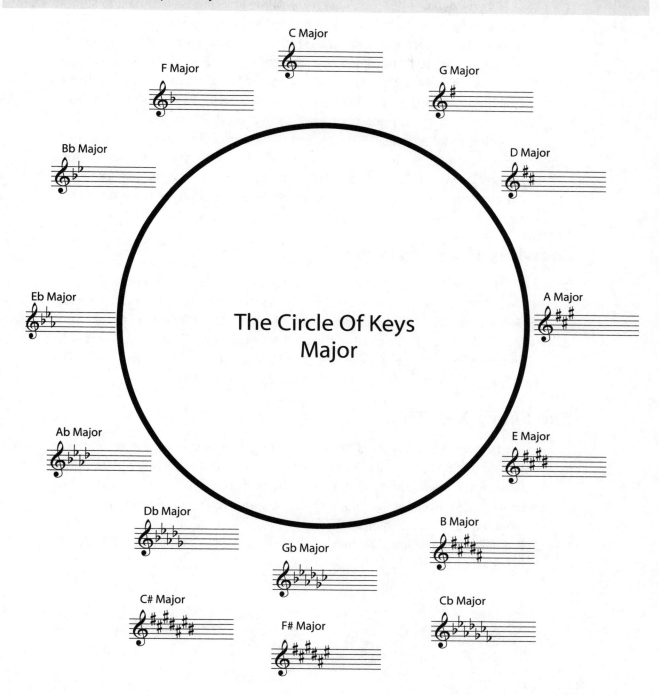

As you can see, the circle starts with the key of C, which has no sharps and no flats. The sharps begin to the right and progress in intervals, each of them five notes away, also called fifths. The flat keys move to the left and progress in intervals of four notes, also called fourths. At the bottom of the circle, three keys occupy the same space as three other keys: G♭ with F♯, C♯ with D♭, and B with C♭. This happens because they are "enharmonic" to each other. If you remember from earlier in this book, an enharmonic is something that sounds the same, but is spelled differently in the scale. All the enharmonic scales will sound exactly the same, yet they use different pitches. As you progress around the circle, either left or right, you'll see that the key signatures add either a flat or a sharp, depending on what side of the circle you're on.

Learning the Key Names

If you stare at the circle of keys long enough you might memorize what each key represents. There are a few tricks that can help you out. On the flat side, the first key is F, which starts with the same letter as the word flat. After that BEAD takes the names of the next four flat keys. That's a handy way to learn some of the keys. However, there are two little "tricks" you can learn for instantly naming a key just from looking at it.

The Sharp Key Trick

For any key that has a sharp in it, naming the key is as simple as following two easy steps. First, find the last sharp (the one all the way to the right). Once you've found and named the note that corresponds to the same line or space the sharp is on, go one note higher, and you've named the key. Look at **FIGURE 10-4**. The last sharp in this key is G♯. Going one note above this is the note A. Three sharps is indeed the correct key signature for the key of A. You can check the trusty circle just to make sure.

FIGURE 10-4
Naming a Sharp
Key

The good news is that this works on every key that has a sharp in it. To find the name of a sharp key:

1. Name the last sharp, the one all the way to the right.
2. Go one note higher than the last sharp, and that's the name!

Easy enough! Unfortunately, it only works when you're looking at a key. If someone asks you "How many sharps are in the key of E major?" this little trick won't get you very far. To answer that kind of question, refer to the circle of keys and the order of sharps and flats.

The Flat Key Trick

The flat keys have their own, different trick for naming them. When you see a piece of music that has flats, find the second to last flat. The name of that flat is the name of your key! This is an easy one. Look at the example in **FIGURE 10-5**. This key has four flats and the second to last flat is A♭. The name of the key with four flats is A♭! This one is an easy trick.

FIGURE 10-5
Naming a Flat
Key

There is one catch, however . . . the key with one flat, F major. Since this key only has one flat, you can't find the second to last flat. In this case, you'll just have to memorize that F has one flat (which is B♭). Shouldn't be too hard! To find the name of a flat key:

1. Find the second to last flat (from the right).
2. The name of the flat note you find is the name of the key.

Just remember the exception: the key of F has one flat and the rule does not work. For the other keys, it works like a charm!

Relative Minor Keys

Up to this point, you have learned solely about major keys and their scales. The circle of keys and those two tricks for naming the keys have all referred to major keys.

The other scale and key that tonal music deals with are the minor scale and key. There is good and bad news. The good news is that all of the minor scales and keys share the same key signatures that you already know. The bad news is that they aren't the same as the major keys! Never fear, there are some easy ways for you to learn the minor keys as well.

Just looking at a key signature won't tell you whether your piece is in the major or the minor key. To find out for sure, you need to investigate the piece itself, not just the signature.

Shared Signatures

Every major key and its corresponding key signature have a dual function. Not only do they indicate a major key, but they also indicate one minor key. The concept is called relative keys and related minor. Simply put, every major scale/key has a minor scale/key hiding inside it. Later in this book, you will learn much more about the minor scale in depth. For now, let's learn how to figure out the name of the minor keys. Figure 10-6 shows the key signature for C major. The exact same key signature can also signify the key of A minor.

How is this possible? You'll get into that in Chapter 12, where you'll get all the dirt on minor scales. For now, just understand that you can look at a key two different ways: from the major and from the minor. Let's look at how to name any minor key from any major key signature.

FIGURE 10-6
Key Signature for
C Major/A Minor

Naming Minor Keys

To name a minor key signature, first name the major key. Once you have found that, you simply count up six notes, or down three—either way, you arrive at the same note. In the case of C major, counting up six notes brings you to the note A. C major and A minor share the same key signature. They are referred to as related keys. When you look at a piece with no sharps or flats in the signature, it may not necessarily be in C major; it could just as easily be in A minor. (To learn how to tell for sure, read Chapters 11 and 12). For now, just work on being able to name minor keys from major key signatures.

When naming a minor key, be careful to look at the key signature when you are doing so. Simply counting up six notes or down three notes may not give you the correct key. If the note you pick has a sharp or a flat in that key, the name of the minor key needs to reflect that. Look at **FIGURE 10-7**. In this case, the sixth note was not just F, but F♯, so the name of the key had to reflect that. The key of A major has a relative minor of F♯ minor.

FIGURE 10-8 is the full circle of keys with both the major and the minor keys listed.

FIGURE 10-7
The Key of A
Major/ F♯ Minor

FIGURE 10-8 The Circle of Keys with Minors

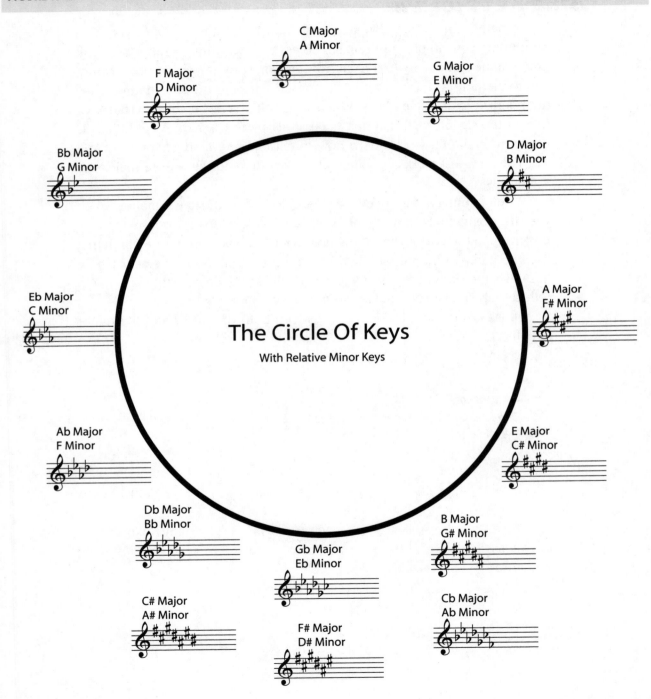

Using Keys for Particular Instruments

Many times, due to how certain instruments work, groups of instruments tend to play in sharp keys more than flat keys or vice versa. This is largely due to issues such as transposition. You may have noticed that

- Strings read in sharp keys more often, and they do so more comfortably.
- Brass and winds read in flat keys more often, and they do so more comfortably.

This is not to say that a string player never reads in flat keys, or that a flute will never read in sharps. Your own experience may mirror this on your own instrument. Ideally, a great musician should be able to read in any key, no matter what. In the study of your instrument, you may have wondered why you don't see certain keys and why you aren't as comfortable in other keys. Now you know why!

When No Key Signature Is Used

There are a few instances where using a key signature may not work. The first is if you are playing or writing music that is atonal—for instance, twentieth-century pieces written by composers such as Berg and Webern. If the music does not follow the tonal system, then key signatures will not work for you. Key signatures aid in playing and reading music based on tonality, which is built around the major and minor scales/keys. If your music does not adhere to this, than use of a key signature won't help.

The other time key signatures aren't used is in jazz writing. Many times, jazz music is so highly chromatic and changes keys so often that using a key signature wouldn't make much sense. Jazz often changes keys on a measure-per-measure basis, making the use of key signatures more of a hindrance than a help. This is not a steadfast rule, however, and you may occasionally see a key signature used in jazz.

Chapter 11
Major Scales

Understanding how music works entails looking at the structure of music and seeing how it ticks. The first step to understanding music is to look at the major scale. The more you understand about music, the better you will read and create music. This chapter introduces you to the major scales.

Scales Defined

You've heard the term many times before. Many of you play scales in some shape or form and don't even know it. They've been mentioned countless times in this book. Now it's time to look more closely at what they are.

A scale is a grouping of notes together that makes a key. Most of the scales that you will encounter have seven different pitches (but a total of eight notes with the repeated octave) in them. Some scales that you'll learn later in the book contain more than seven notes, and some less. The bread and butter definition of a scale is that it's a series of eight notes (seven different pitches) that start and end on the same note, which is also called the root. The root names the scale. If a scale starts and ends on C, the root is C and the scale's name is either C major or C minor. Since this chapter focuses on major scales, let's look at a very basic C major scale in **FIGURE 11-1**.

 FIGURE 11-1 C Major Scale

TRACK 40

As you can see, the scale starts and ends on C and progresses up every note in order. Since C major contains no sharps and no flats, it's an easy scale to understand and remember. On the piano, it's simply all the white notes. The C scale contains seven different notes: C, D, E, F, G, A, and B. The last C isn't counted, as it's just a repeated note. The major scale has eight notes in total, though.

What makes this a major scale? The first definition as to why it's major is because it sounds major. Don't take this for granted! The sound of scales is everything! While there are twenty-four different major scales, they all sound like major scales. They will sound so much like major scales that you'll easily be able to recognize them when you hear them. Just as you'll never mistake the melody for "Happy Birthday" with "Jingle Bells," you'll never mistake a major scale for anything else.

The other reason that it's a major scale is that the construction of the scale follows a pattern. The pattern it follows is the same pattern that all major scales follow. This is why they sound the same; they are built from the same stuff.

Basic Intervals

An interval is the distance between any two musical notes. Intervals can be big or small depending on the notes themselves. Intervals are how musicians deconstruct music into its smallest parts. The first two intervals you need to know are the two smallest intervals that music has. Understanding these intervals will allow you to deconstruct the major scale and understand its inner workings.

First is the half step. The half step is the smallest interval in our system of music. A half step is the distance between C and C#. Take a look at a piano to understand a half step. On the piano, a half step interval is the distance from any key to the next closest key (see **FIGURE 11-2**). This can mean a white key to a black key, a black key to a white key, or a white key to a white key in certain instances.

FIGURE 11-2 Half Steps on the Piano

TRACK 41

Half Step Intervals

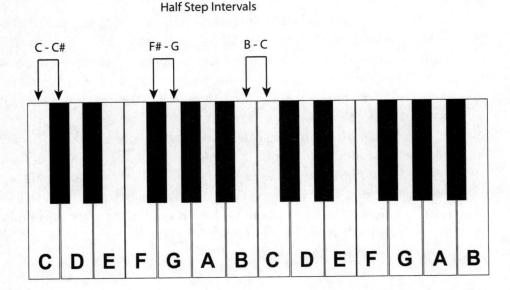

FACT

Those of you who are movie buffs may already recognize a very common interval: The memorable theme from *Jaws* uses a very low half step interval.

A whole step is next. A whole step is simply twice as large as a half step. To make a whole step, simply proceed up two half steps—two half steps equal a whole step. **FIGURE 11-3** shows a few whole steps on the piano.

FIGURE 11-3 Whole Steps on the Piano

TRACK 42   Whole Step Intervals

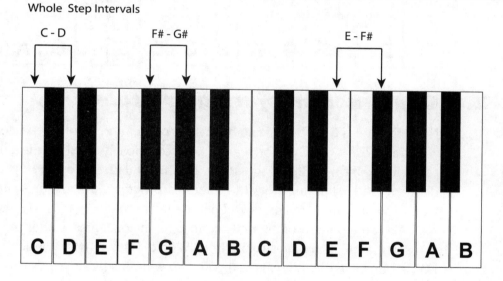

You need to watch out for something known as natural half steps. On the piano, between B and C and between E and F exists something called a natural half step. With these notes, there isn't a black key sharp/flat between them. Usually on the piano when you progress from a white key to an adjacent white key it's a whole step. Be aware that from B to C and from E to F are only half step intervals, even though they move through letter names. Usually, half steps go from naturals to sharps, sharps to naturals, or flats to naturals. This holds true for all instruments, not just piano. When working with music and intervals, don't get trapped by this common pitfall! Remember, B to C and E to F = half step. That almost rhymes!

FIGURE 11-4 The Natural Half Steps on the Piano

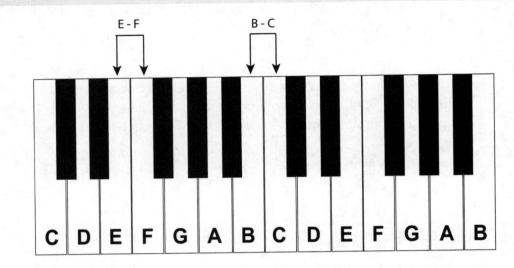

The Construction of a Major Scale

Now that you have a better understanding of half and whole step intervals, you can look at the C major scale a bit more closely. Look at the C major scale in **FIGURE 11-5**. Below the scale, the intervals between the notes are defined. Understanding how the intervals progress in a major scale will teach you not only C major, but all of the major scales.

This same pattern of intervals defines all major scales. Under the scale you see the following intervals: Whole, Whole, Half, Whole, Whole, Whole, Half. Abbreviate the intervals and come up with this formula:

WWHWWWH

FIGURE 11-5 C Major Scale with Intervals

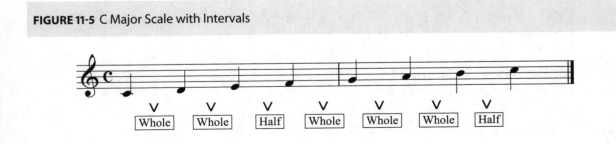

Test the Formula

Let's test this formula a few times. **FIGURE 11-6** shows a few major scales written out in different keys. Play through them to hear that they sound like major scales. Below the scales, there is room for you to write in the intervals. Go ahead and write them in pencil.

FIGURE 11-6 Adding Intervals to Major Scales

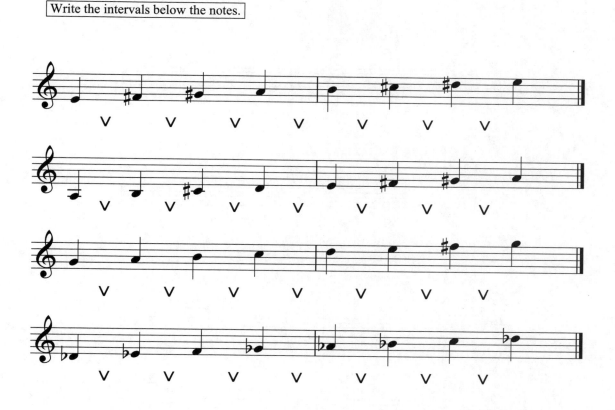

Notice how each scale follows the same pattern of **WWHWWWH**. Remember that structurally each major scale is exactly the same. The notes that it takes to make each scale will always be different, because no two major scales use the exact same notes, but the intervals between those notes are always constant.

FIGURE 11-7 Scale Practice Exercise

Using the space provided, spell out major scales using the WWHWWWH formula.

Practice Scales

Writing scales on your own is good practice for understanding how they work. In **FIGURE 11-7**, the first note of each major scale is provided. Follow the formula to figure out each of the rest of the notes in the scales. Here are a few tips to make sure you write them accurately.

- Each scale will contain eight notes, including the repeated root of the scale.
- Each scale will use each letter of the musical alphabet only once.
- All major scales follow the same pattern of **WWHWWWH** intervals.
- Scales use either flats or sharps, never both.

Once you've written them in, play them! Always play your work to check it. Music theory isn't about abstract theory and patterns, it's about learning how to create sound. So above all else, make sure that you check your work with your instrument and your ears.

You should now have a decent handle on how to spell and identify scales. Now, why do you need to know them? And how do they fit into the overall picture of music?

Musical DNA

In the history of music education, no word instills as much fear as scales. Too many musicians have had to suffer through repetitive, boring scale practice. What's worse is that you're rarely told why you're learning them and what benefit they will have for your playing.

Scales are the building blocks of tonal music. Think of scales as musical DNA. By itself, a scale is a dead thing. If you think of scales starting and ending on the same note, progressing up and down, they don't sound too impressive. But once you know a scale, you're free to reorder it and combine it any way you choose. Simply, scales provide the basis for melody and harmony. Let's look at some famous examples of how simple scales can be organized into melodies. Every melody you've heard in your life is part of some scale, and many of them come from the commonly used major scale. **FIGURE 11-8** is an example from Bach that many of you will recognize.

FIGURE 11-8 Bach Example

TRACK 43

As you can see from the key signature, this example is in the key of G. Notice how the melody in the treble clef is made up solely of notes from the G major scale (G A B C D E F♯ G). Bach simply reorganizes the dry scale into small melodies. All of the notes in this piece come from the G major scale. As you can see from this simple piece, the scale can go a long way. **FIGURE 11-9** is another example of a melody you know that comes from a scale—it's the classic melody "Oh Susanna." Again, look at the melody. All of the notes come from a basic major scale; in this case, looking at the key signature shows us that this melody is in F major (F G A B♭ C D E F).

FIGURE 11-9 "Oh Susanna"

TRACK 44

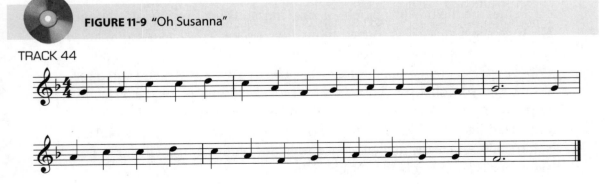

Those are just two examples of major scale melodies. There are hundreds of melodies based on major scales. As your ear progresses, you'll be able to pick them out just by listening. Soon enough, you'll be able to pick out a major scale a mile away—that is, if you can't already. Here are a few other notable examples of major scale melodies:

- Jingle Bells
- Happy Birthday
- Over the Rainbow
- This Land Is Your Land
- Do-Re-Mi (*Sound of Music*)

Look through the examples in this book. See if you can identify whether the examples are written in major scales or not. Also, play the CD that accompanies this book. Close your eyes and hear the melodies on the CD and see if you can pick out some major scale melodies. It's easier than you think. Major scales have been known to remind people of happy sounds.

Scales and Harmony

As you now know, scales are successions of notes. You can combine single-note scales in various ways to make infinite numbers of melodies. For those of you who play single-note instruments—i.e., instruments that can only play one note at a time—this is how you have viewed much of music: one note at a time.

Instruments that can play more than one note at a time, mainly piano and guitar, are able to play "harmony," which is also referred to as chords. A chord is at least three notes played together at the same time. Chords are covered in much greater detail in Chapter 14, but for now you need to know a few basics about chords.

Stacked Scales

If you take the notes from a scale and start to play them together, you begin to experience some harmony. If you were to sit down at a piano and play in the key of C major, randomly playing groupings of three notes, you would stumble upon a couple of things:

- Certain combinations of notes will sound good to you.
- Certain combinations of notes will not sound good to you.

As you'll learn later in the book, there is a reason why certain groupings of notes sound good and other ones don't. The groupings you played randomly that sounded good and pleasing to your ear are likely chords, or triads. The groupings that didn't sound good were likely not chords.

Triads

If you were to spell out a scale and play the first, third, and fifth notes together, you would be playing a triad. It's called a triad not only because it has three notes in it but also because each note is three notes apart. Tri is also the Greek word for "three." In music, the first note is always counted as one. **FIGURE 11-10** shows a triad from the C major scale.

FIGURE 11-10 C Major Triad

TRACK 45

As you can see—and, more importantly, hear—these notes sound great together. From a simple scale, you could select these notes and play them together to form a pleasing harmony. This is where a great deal of music comes from—single notes make the melodies, while the combined notes form the chords that make harmony. Better yet, it can all be done with one simple formula: **WWHWWWH**. The major scale gives us all that. Scales are indeed multifaceted.

Applying Scales in Practice

Hopefully, by this point you understand the importance of scales. They are a key building block for music. So how can knowing scales make you a better reader? For theory to be practical, you have to be able to use it and apply it.

Sequences and Patterns

Since melodies are often made out of scales, practicing scales and knowing them fluently on your instrument will make reading easier. As you become familiar with the different musical keys on your instrument, playing and reading in those keys becomes less work. Let's look at some different ways that you can practice scales. One such way is by practicing scale sequences. A sequence is a term taken from mathematics. A sequence is simply a pattern of numbers such as 1-2-3, 2-3-4, or 3-4-5. It's simply any order of numbers that follows some sort of pattern. How does this apply to music? If you number each note of a major scale, you can easily apply some sequences to your scales. Let's take a look at a simple one in **FIGURE 11-11**.

FIGURE 11-11 Sequence Number 1

TRACK 46

Each scale tone in **FIGURE 11-11** is numbered, and the notes have been ordered in a simple pattern sequence. The result is a fairly neat sound. You could keep playing this pattern to the ends of your instrument, both ascending and descending. Not only do sequences break up the monotony of practicing scales, composers have been known to employ sequences in their music from time to time. If you can spot them while reading, you'll breeze right through those sections.

A sequence can be anything. Spend sometime playing pattern scales and sequences. **FIGURE 11-12** is an example with a bunch of common sequences. But in these examples, only the first iteration is provided. For practice, write out the rest of the notes—continue the pattern for each scale to construct the full sequence. Practice playing each sequence.

FIGURE 11-12 More Example Sequences

TRACK 47

Transposing

All of the example sequences you have seen so far have been in the key of C major. What if you'd like to play them in other keys? All you have to do is transpose the numerical sequence to another scale. Since every scale is basically the same because all major scales share the same intervals, a 1-2-3-4-5 sequence just means that you play the first, second, third, fourth, and fifth notes of that scale. In theory, a sequence does not refer to any key, as the numbers are universal to all keys. Let's take a simple sequence and see how that same sequence can be applied to different keys (see **FIGURE 11-13**). As you can see, there is nothing to transposing if you know your scales!

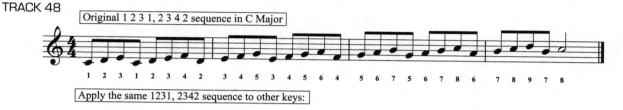

FIGURE 11-13 Sequence Transposition

TRACK 48

It is worth your while to practice all the major keys, starting from every note on your instrument. Now that you know how to easily construct the scales and apply the sequences, come up with some interesting variations and patterns to practice. Remember, if you know all your major scales up and down and in a few different patterns, then reading in different keys will be no problem for you.

Chapter 12

Beyond Major Scales: The Minor Scale

The basic language of music is derived from two scales: major and minor. Commonly, the major scales are thought of as "happy" scales, while their counterparts, the minor scales, are "darker" and more melancholy. The minor scale is closely related to the major scale and is an essential element of reading and making music.

Not Major, Minor

By this point, you have learned a lot about the major scale. The major scale is an essential, commonly used musical scale. It represents a certain "color" or type of sound. The minor scale is a different color; a darker sound. It's also the "other" main musical scale. As a musician, you'll encounter the minor scale often.

The minor scale is an alternative to the major scale, yielding a different musical color than the major scale. Certain pieces can convey moods and feelings based on the key and type of scale they're written in. A great example of this is Looney Tunes soundtrack music. Yes, Bugs Bunny! The next time you watch one of these cartoons, listen closely to the background music. You'll find major keys for happy, bright events and minor keys for the darker and more serious moments. It's not just cartoons; film music often uses the same basic contrast of minor versus major. **FIGURE 12-1** is an example from Beethoven's Fifth Symphony. Even if you don't like or know much about classical music, you'll know this famous theme.

FIGURE 12-1 Beethoven's Fifth Symphony Theme

TRACK 49

That strong melody is made from the C minor scale. Hear how it has a certain "weight" and feeling that you don't get with the major scales. Now that you've heard the scale in action, let's look at where it comes from and how minor scales are constructed.

FACT

The plain melody of Beethoven's Fifth Symphony does not scream C minor. The rest of the movement and other parts do identify the key definitively as C minor, but this example by itself could just as easily be read in three flats of E♭ major. The context of the rest of the movement is important to note for identifying the key of the piece.

In the last chapter, you learned about basic whole and half steps. Using that information, you were able to construct a major scale using the formula **WWHWWWH**. One formula gave you every major scale possible and made it easy for you to figure out the notes in all of the keys.

The minor scale also uses a pattern of whole and half steps. Luckily for you, virtually all the scales in the musical universe use some combination of whole and half steps. The minor scale is constructed using this pattern: **WHWWHWW**. Let's put the formula to use. **FIGURE 12-2** is an example of a C minor scale using this interval formula.

FIGURE 12-2 C Minor Scale Construction

By using the intervals, you can construct any minor scale you choose. Major and minor scales are the two most important scales to know. There are more scales besides these two, but as you will see later in this book, all of the other scales will relate to either the major or minor scale. Knowing these two scales intimately will equip you for anything that comes your way.

Where Minor Actually Comes From

It's time to 'fess up. The formula you just learned (**WHWWHWW**) is a quick and easy way to spell out any minor scale. But this does not explain the true origins of the minor scale. Simply, the minor scale is something known as a mode.

A mode is what you get any time you play a major scale but start and end somewhere other than the root. It uses the exact same notes, just reorganized. Modes are covered in greater detail in Chapter 18. The first mode that you learn is the minor scale. That's right—the minor scale lives inside of a major scale; you just have to learn to see it.

Relative Minor Keys

If you're shaking your head about what modes are, here is a concrete example. Let's start with the old standby, the C major scale (see **FIGURE 12-3**).

FIGURE 12-3 C Major Scale

What makes this a C major scale is not only the construction of the intervals, but the fact that it starts and ends on C. You could say that this scale is "centered" around the note C. Whenever you're in a key, the root of the scale—that is, the note that gives the scale its name—is the most important note. To our ears, that note has a certain amount of weight; it sounds complete when you stop there.

When the starting point of the scale is changed, you get a mode. The minor scale is simply a mode of the major scale. If you play a major scale from the sixth note, you are playing a minor scale. Let's use the C major scale again. The sixth note is A. By taking the notes from the C major scale and starting on A you get the scale in **FIGURE 12-4**.

FIGURE 12-4 A Minor Scale

TRACK 50

This is an A minor scale. All of the notes come from the key of C major, yet by reordering them this way they become a minor scale. This is called a relative minor key. Every major key has a related minor key inside of it. If you remember the circle of keys from **FIGURE 10-8**, each of the major keys also had a minor key attached to it. You'll see that C major and A minor sit together on the same spot of the circle.

Standing Alone

So the minor scale is a mode. There happen to be modes on each and every note of the major scale, seven different modes with seven different names. The minor scale has elevated itself beyond just a mode. It's a full-fledged key; it stands alone from the other modes that are more like accessories and ornamental sounds. The key of A minor is not necessarily related to C major. This is what you need to learn to separate. Yes, A minor comes from C major. Yes, it contains the same notes. However, they are not the same thing. This isn't chemistry. In musical terms, if they sound different, they are different. Since the key of C major and the key of A minor sound different from each other, they are treated as different things.

Knowing that C major and A minor are related only helps you name keys based on looking at a key signature. For example, looking at the key signature in **FIGURE 12-5** tells you that this is either C major or A minor. You can't be sure what it is unless you look at the music itself and see other aspects of the harmony. (You will learn this skill later in the book as well.)

FIGURE 12-5 Key Signature

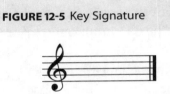

Parallel Minor Keys

Relative minor keys are useful in understanding key signatures and the nature of where minor scales come from. What relative keys don't tell you is the difference between major and minor keys that share the same root, such as C major and C minor. These are called parallel keys—keys that share the root but are different scales. To understand how to move from any major scale to any minor scale sharing the same root, look at the notes of the C major scale:

C D E F G A B C

Now look at the notes of the C minor scale:

C D E♭ F G A♭ B♭ C

Look closely: What's different between these two scales? From C major, three notes have been lowered with flats: E, A, and B have been changed to E♭, A♭, and B♭. This is essential. If you number the tones in the scale, you can see that the third, sixth, and seventh tones of the major scale were lowered one half step down to make a minor scale. This isn't just for one key; this affects all the keys! To transform any major scale into a minor scale of the same name/root, simply lower the third, sixth, and seventh tones one half step down.

You can also use the formula of whole and half intervals that you learned about in the first section of this chapter. You'll find that as you progress with music theory, most everything is a derivation of the major scale. In either case, it's nice to know a few different ways to the same answer.

Basic Minor Harmony

In the last chapter, you learned to take the first, third, and fifth tones from the major scale and form a triad. This carries over to the minor scales as well. By simply playing these three notes together (see **FIGURE 12-6**), you can hear a C minor triad, or, as it's commonly known, a C minor chord.

 FIGURE 12-6 C Minor Triad

TRACK 51

When you compare the C major chord in the last chapter to the C minor chord, you'll notice a few things. First, each of the chords contains some form of the notes C E G. Both chords contain the notes C and G exactly. The only difference is that a C major chord has a third of E and the C minor chord contains a third of E♭. This holds true for each chord relationship when you switch from major to minor and retain the same root.

To formulate this into a rule: To change a major chord to a minor chord, lower the third of the major chord down one half step. In the case of C major it worked like this: The C major chord is C E G and the C minor chord is C

E♭ G. This idea will be important to remember when you get to Chapter 15 on harmony. For now, just be aware of it; it's a very convenient way to understand chords and their relationships to each other.

The Variant Scales of Minor

The minor scale we have dealt with is considered the basic or "natural" minor scale. Throughout the evolution and history of music, the minor scale has been adapted to better suit the melody and harmony of the time. Two variations of the minor scale are so prevalent that they have emerged as their own scales. The two variations are the harmonic and melodic minor scales. Since these scales appear as adjuncts to or replacements for the minor scale, it's important to know them. Understanding the construction and practice of these scales will be important to understanding harmony and chords (in Chapters 15, 16, and 17).

Harmonic Minor

Harmonic minor is the first variation of the minor scale you should know. It's a simple change of a basic minor scale. To form the harmonic minor scale, simply take a minor scale and raise the seventh note up one half step (see **FIGURE 12-7**).

FIGURE 12-7 Natural Minor to Harmonic Minor

TRACK 52

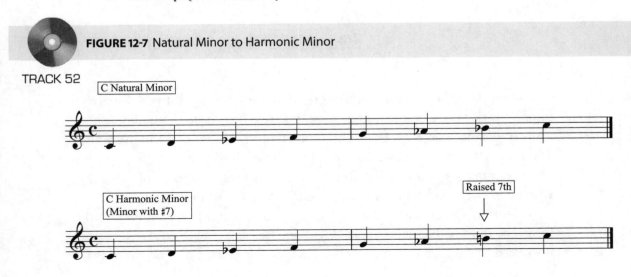

Harmonic minor gives composers an option for varying the sound of the minor scale to create a slightly different harmony. Making the change to the seventh scale degree, some of the chords change, and the harmony is affected. This is why it's called harmonic minor. Melodically, you are left with an ugly scale to work with. There is a large gap between the sixth and seventh tones that can be melodically awkward, to say the least. To work around this, composers created yet another scale to solve this dilemma: the melodic minor scale.

Melodic Minor

To fix the strange sound that the harmonic minor scale makes, the melodic minor scale was born. The melodic minor scale is made by raising the sixth and seventh tones of a natural minor scale up one half step each (see **FIGURE 12-8**).

FIGURE 12-8 Natural Minor to Melodic Minor

TRACK 53

The whole point of the melodic minor scale is to smooth out the skip in the harmonic minor scale. The raised seventh tone in harmonic minor is crucial to minor scale harmony, but the scale itself sounds strange. By raising the sixth as well, the melodic minor scale works better for melodies and harmonies. This is why it's called the melodic minor scale. Both the harmonic and melodic minor scales fall under the umbrella of basic music theory, which is important to understand to make sense of reading music. Now that you know how to construct them, try to write them out in every key and learn to play them on your instrument.

Playing Minor Scales

So far you have learned about three different minor scales in this chapter: natural minor, harmonic minor, and melodic minor. The only "real" scale is the natural minor scale. The other scales—harmonic and melodic— are scales that appeared in the music of great composers first and were analyzed and lumped as scales later by theorists.

Classical musicians typically practice minor scales by playing melodic minor as the scale ascends and natural minor as the scale descends (see **FIGURE 12-9**). This is sometimes how the scales appear, but there is no steadfast rule. Harmonic minor is rarely practiced this way, as it's more of a harmonic tool and not a melodic one.

 FIGURE 12-9 Classical Minor Scales

TRACK 54

In contemporary music, the minor scales exist on their own, as separate scales. Jazz makes frequent use of the melodic minor scale, while pop music virtually ignores harmonic and melodic minor in favor of natural minor. If you play jazz, practicing all three forms of the minor scale will be useful to you, as jazz improvisation utilizes all the scales individually.

As with the major scale, minor scale sequences are a valuable practice aid. Just as you do with the major scale—or with any scale—you can apply numerical sequences to organize and practice the minor scales. Try some sequences and patterns when you practice. Go back to Chapter 10 and convert the major scale sequences to minor scale sequences now that you know how to do it.

Learning to Identify Minor Keys

If you've never analyzed music before, looking at a piece of music and deciphering what key it is in is a huge undertaking. The key signature alone won't give you the answer. The old rules such as "Look at the first and the last note of the piece" work so infrequently, it's almost best to ignore them. How can you learn to look at a piece and figure out if you're in major or minor? Unless you've memorized every possible combination of notes that make scales, you're going to rely on the key signatures to give you a ballpark idea of what key you're in.

Unfortunately, key signatures only give you so much information. You know that, because of relative key signatures, there are two possible keys for each signature: e.g., C major and A minor share the same key signature. How do you know which is which?

No one rule works every single time for determining the key a piece is in. While there are tricks you can use to help you figure it out, there are many exceptions in music.

How Major Keys Look

The simplest way to tell if you're in a major key is to look at the piece itself. If the piece contains no accidentals other than the original key signature, then it probably is in major. This is because the major scale is perfect and needs no alterations to work effectively.

How Minor Keys Look

Minor keys require something extra to make them "work," in a classical sense. Both the harmonic and melodic minor scales contain the raised seventh tone, which makes the harmony of the minor scale work. The raised seventh tone is also referred to as a leading tone, because it leads up the root of the scale so strongly. The good news is that almost 99.99999 percent of pieces in minor keys need a leading tone (raised seventh). Without the leading tone, the harmony that your ear expects won't be there. To get this leading tone, the scale must be altered—a note in the key signature will be changed to something else. A major scale doesn't have to do this. A minor scale does. This is going to make it easier to recognize minor keys.

Finding Leading Tones

Leading tones are very easy to name. They are always one half step below the root of the minor scale. For example, in the key of A minor, the leading tone is G♯. As you may remember, the key of A minor has no sharps or flats in its key signature. Regardless of this, a piece in the key of A minor is going to be littered with G♯s. Simply looking for this leading tone will help you find the minor key if it's used.

Here is a rundown:

1. Figure out what keys the piece could be in, based on the key signature. For example, two ♯s could be D major or B minor.
2. Name the minor leading tone. The key of B minor has a leading tone of A♯. (Leading tones are one half step below the roots.)
3. Look in your piece for the leading tone. If you can find it, the piece is in minor. If you can't, it is in major.

FIGURE 12-10 is an example in the key of D minor. The key signature is one ♭, which could be F major or D minor. This famous excerpt is from Bach's Toccata and Fugue in D Minor. The C♯ leading tone gave this one away as being D minor (so did the title of the piece!). As you see more pieces like this, you will learn to spot the leading tones quickly.

FIGURE 12-10 Identifying a Minor Key

Leading Tones Highlighted

Holes in This Theory

This trick works. But, like every other theory rule you're going to learn, it's far from perfect. There are a few things that could mess it up. First, music changes key. While you may be able to fulfill the rules for a short period of time, it may not last long enough to be useful. Second, not all music uses a key signature. There are so many variables here. The good news is that it does work . . . most of the time. Also, composers are free to use accidentals whenever they want to. Usually there is a system at play when you see accidentals. In any case, you'll be able to get a lot of mileage out of this trick for identifying major and minor pieces. However, there is no substitute for real musical analysis, and that involves looking at all the parts, not just the leading tones.

Speaking of analysis, it's time to learn more about the tools that you'll need to understand everything about music theory. Intervals, here we come!

Chapter 13

Space and Distance: Musical Intervals

One of the first steps to understanding music theory is learning some basic musical intervals. Simple half and whole steps became the basis for spelling and understanding major and minor scales. Understanding the rest of the intervals will give you the tools to unlock everything you ever wanted to know about music.

What Is an Interval?

The term interval is not exclusive to music. An interval is loosely defined as a measure between events; this can be a distance of physical space or time. In music, the term applies to the distance between any two musical notes. Intervals consist of two aspects, numeric size and quality or type. You have already learned about the two simplest intervals: the whole step and the half step. By using whole and half steps, you were able to construct a whole bunch of scales! In order to understand and unlock chords and harmony, you'll need to understand intervals. To start with, let's look at a simple major scale and define the intervals so that you get used to the lingo involved.

Interval Weirdness

Music theory has many weird quirks and exceptions. Intervals are a very good example of this. As you progress through this chapter and the rest of the book, remember that music theory is a way to understand music that's already been written. Theory comes after the music itself. Music doesn't follow theory; theory describes music. Therefore, it is inevitable that you'll encounter broken rules and other confusing aspects. In relation to intervals, theorists have had to come up with a system to name the musical distance between any two notes. This system has to deal with one major obstacle: enharmonics! As you'll see through this chapter, intervals have to differentiate between notes that sound the same but are written with different pitch names. You'll see some conventions that make sense, and you'll need to learn the exceptions. Let's start with the common major scale.

Intervals in a Major Scale

FIGURE 13-1 is a major scale with its intervals. The first thing that you should note is that the intervals are being measured from the root of C to each of the other notes. The single most frequent mistake students make when measuring intervals is forgetting to count the first note as one. You must always count the note that you are starting from as one and proceed forward. From the C major scale, the following intervals result:

FIGURE 13-1 Intervals in a C Major Scale

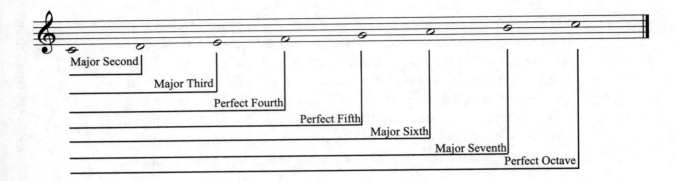

- C - D = Major Second
- C - E = Major Third
- C - F = Perfect Fourth
- C - G = Perfect Fifth
- C - A = Major Sixth
- C - B = Major Seventh
- C - C = Perfect Octave

The first time you look at this listing, it's undoubtedly confusing. It's pretty easy to deduce that the intervals that are called major come from the major scale. What about the perfect intervals? What makes them so perfect? The first thing to note here is that only seven intervals are defined. There are five other chromatic notes that need to be named. Let's take a look at a C minor scale, which will introduce a few more notes and intervals.

Intervals in a Minor Scale

Let's look at all the intervals from a C minor scale (see **FIGURE 13-2**). Since the same root of C is used for both the major scale in the previous example and the minor scale here, you can easily see what's the same and what's not. Here is how the intervals break down for this scale:

FIGURE 13-2 Intervals in a C Minor Scale

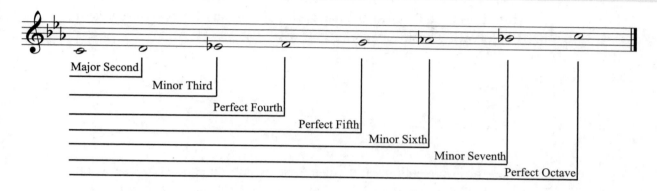

- C - D = Major Second
- C - E♭ = Minor Third
- C - F = Perfect Fourth
- C - G = Perfect Fifth
- C - A♭ = Minor Sixth
- C - B♭ = Minor Seventh
- C - C = Perfect Octave

Compare these two sets of intervals. To start with, from C major to C minor the fourth and fifth notes didn't change; they retained their title of perfect. Maybe they are perfect because they are the same in both scales? The "official" answer to that one is coming soon. Every interval that was major in the major scale and changed in the minor scale got the title of minor interval (third, sixth, and seventh).

The second note is a bit confusing. It's the same for both C major and C minor. The other notes that were the same for both scales (F and G) were designated as "perfect." Why isn't the second interval perfect as well? Here is the first of the irregularities of intervals!

Certain intervals stayed the same, while others changed. So far you have encountered major, minor, and perfect intervals. Why do certain intervals get the names that they do? It's time to break all the intervals down by type so you can learn the convention of what's used where and why. Once you get used to it, it's not difficult.

Basic Interval Types

Let's break down in detail all the categories of intervals. Intervals are broken into the following basic categories:

- Major
- Minor
- Perfect

There are conventions and rules as to which categories to use when and why. Let's talk about each interval type separately and give examples to help you understand them.

Major

Major intervals can only be used for the following intervals: seconds, thirds, sixths, and sevenths. It is true that all of the major intervals can be found in the major scale, and that's a decent way to find out how to spell them if you're stuck. **FIGURE 13-3** shows a bunch of examples of major intervals.

FIGURE 13-3 Major Intervals

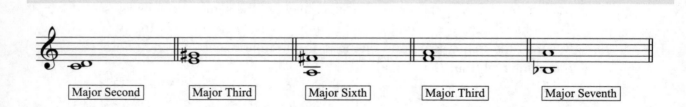

| Major Second | Major Third | Major Sixth | Major Third | Major Seventh |

When you learn to count intervals, you must keep track of the key signature for the key you are in. This is the easiest way to be sure you are spelling the interval with the correct accidentals. You could break down any interval by the number of half steps it contains—although this is only helpful on smaller intervals. Knowing scales and key signatures is the most efficient way to boost your interval knowledge.

Minor

Minor intervals are used for seconds, thirds, sixths, and sevenths (see **FIGURE 13-4**). Minor intervals are always a half step smaller than major intervals with the same number. A minor second is the smallest interval: The halfstep is a minor second. Minor intervals are found in the minor scale with the notable exception of the second, which is major in both the major and the minor scale. The reason that you call the distance between the first and second notes in both major and minor scales a major second is that major only designates that the interval is larger. There is a whole step between the first and second notes of both scales. You need to leave room to name the smaller interval, the half step. We give that interval the designation minor simply because it's smaller. This may lead to some confusion in the early stages, but remember that intervals have the Herculean task of trying to name every possible distance between any two notes.

FIGURE 13-4 Minor Intervals

| Minor Second | Minor Sixth | Minor Seventh | Minor Third | Minor Sixth |

Perfect

Perfect intervals are a special breed of intervals. Perfect intervals refer to a certain selected group of notes: unisons, fourths, fifths, and octaves (see **FIGURE 13-5**). Even though a unison isn't an interval, it's still considered perfect. You noticed when you compared the major and minor scales that the fourth and fifth didn't change from scale to scale. They remained perfectly in place.

FIGURE 13-5 Perfect Intervals

| Perfect Unison | Perfect Fourth | Perfect Fifth | Perfect Octave | Perfect Fourth |

The term perfect does not refer to scales. It comes from the musical overtone series. As physical waves of sound, perfect intervals ring in a special way that other intervals do not. It's an interesting study—unfortunately, one beyond the scope of this book.

Tritones

The tritone is a special interval. A tritone is a half step between the perfect fourth and the perfect fifth. It's called the tritone because it's three whole steps higher than any root (see **FIGURE 13-6**). It's also the perfect halfway point if the scale is divided in half. In the key of C major, a tritone is from C to F♯/G♭. (The spelling is inconsequential; you'll arrive at the same sound.)

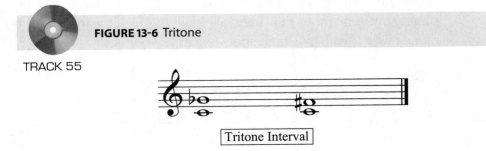

FIGURE 13-6 Tritone

TRACK 55

Tritone Interval

The tritone isn't exactly the most pleasant of sounds. Play it and you'll see. In music history, it was the "never play" interval. It went by many names, one of which was "the devil in music," as its use suggested demonic possession by the composer. The tritone was considered the most caustic and dissonant interval. Composers never purposely wrote that interval. Music history has moved past that extreme thinking, and the tritone is used in modern music.

With perfect, major, minor, and the tritone, you have gotten through all the chromatic intervals. The remaining intervals are more theoretical than anything else.

Enharmonic and Chromatic Intervals

The basic intervals of music are major, minor, and perfect. If you stopped there you would have more than just a cursory understanding of intervals; you could do more than just get by. There are two more types of intervals that deal with the issue of enharmonic spellings of notes and other such anomalies: augmented and diminished intervals.

As you know, the interval of C - E♭ and C - D♯ sound exactly the same. The only thing that's different is the spelling of the D♯ and the E♭. If you remember, that's called an enharmonic.

Now, the spelling of that interval will change as the note changes its name—this is regardless of whether or not they "sound" exactly the same. For example, if the interval is spelled C - E♭ the interval is called a minor third. If the interval is spelled C - D♯ you can't call it a minor third anymore. Third intervals are reserved for intervals of three notes (C to E). Since this interval is from C to D, it must be called a second of some sort. In this case, the correct name is an augmented second. Enharmonic spellings give birth to the need for terms such as augmented and diminished intervals.

Augmented

An augmented interval is any interval that is larger than major or perfect. **FIGURE 13-7** shows a few examples of augmented intervals.

FIGURE 13-7 Augmented Intervals

| Augmented Second | Augmented Third | Augmented Fourth | Augmented Fifth | Augmented Sixth |

Traditionally, you can only augment a second, third, fourth, fifth, or sixth interval. Use augmented intervals when the notes are spelled in an unusual way and you have to adhere to the rule of "It's three notes apart, so I must call it some sort of third, but it's larger than a major third." The deciding factor in all of this is how the interval is spelled on paper. Look for the distance between the notes and use that as your guide. Again, augmented intervals are used when it's too large to be called major or perfect.

Diminished

Diminished intervals are more specialized. A diminished interval names an interval that was made smaller. Typically, diminished intervals are only used to make the perfect intervals smaller. In reality, this is just another spelling convention more than anything else. You can make a fourth or a fifth diminished by lowering any of the perfect intervals one half step. The tritone that you learned about is also a diminished fifth.

Chromatic Intervals

Let's now look at a full chart of every possible interval and enharmonic spelling in one octave to show you how all of this lays out (see **FIGURE 13-8**).

FIGURE 13-8 Chromatic Intervals

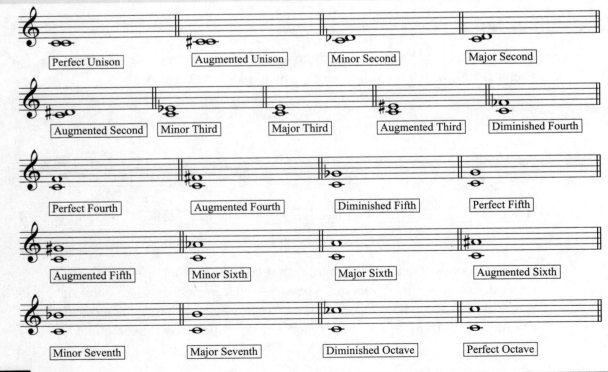

Here is another way to understand intervals. If the top note of the interval exists in the major scale of the bottom note, the interval is major or perfect. If not, it's minor, diminished, or augmented. Here is a little chart to help you. An arrow in either direction indicates movement of a half step.

Diminished ← Minor ← Major → Augmented

Diminished ← Perfect → Augmented

Inverted and Extended Intervals

How far is it from C to G? You might say a perfect fifth. You might be right. However, what if the interval went down? What if the C were written higher on the staff than the G? Would it still be a perfect fifth? In this case, it would actually be a perfect fourth.

So far, this text has dealt with ascending intervals. But what happens when you read an interval down? When you name any interval, such as C to G, you must specify whether it's an ascending interval or a descending interval. If the interval ascends, no worries, you've been trained to handle that—no problem. On the other hand, if the interval descends, it's not spelled the same way. A fifth interval, when flipped around, is not a fifth anymore. This is because the musical scale is not symmetric.

Interval Inversion

Any interval that ascends can be inverted (flipped upside down). Let's look at the example of C - G from the last section (see **FIGURE 13-9**). When you flip the perfect fifth it becomes a perfect fourth. Wouldn't it be great if there were a system to help you invert any interval? Thankfully, there is an easy way to do this. We are going to use a rule called the rule of nine.

FIGURE 13-9 Inverted Intervals

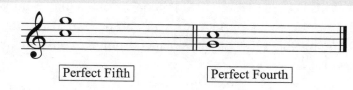

Perfect Fifth   Perfect Fourth

The Rule of Nine

The rule of nine is defined as follows: When any interval is inverted, the sum of the ascending and descending intervals must add up to nine. Using the first example, the interval from C to G is a perfect fifth. The interval from G to C is a perfect fourth. When you add up five and four, you get nine. Let's test this out in a few notation examples (see **FIGURE 13-10**). What's the inversion of a third? It's a sixth, because three and six add to nine. This works on any interval.

FIGURE 13-10 Inverted Intervals and the Rule of Nine

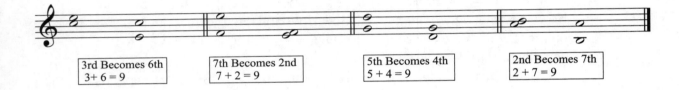

| 3rd Becomes 6th | 7th Becomes 2nd | 5th Becomes 4th | 2nd Becomes 7th |
| 3+ 6 = 9 | 7 + 2 = 9 | 5 + 4 = 9 | 2 + 7 = 9 |

Inverted Qualities

When using the rule of nine, it's easy to flip the intervals over and get the correct inversion. But the type of interval, or quality of the interval, also changes as you invert them. The rule of nine tells us the name of the interval numerically, but the type of interval that it becomes (major, minor, perfect) will change as intervals are flipped over. The answer to this problem has a simple solution. Here is what happens to interval qualities when the intervals invert:

- If the interval was major, it becomes minor when inverted.
- If the interval was minor, it becomes major when inverted.
- If the interval was perfect, it remains perfect when inverted.

This is easy to remember. Major becomes minor, minor becomes major, and perfect stays perfect. As you can see, by using the rule of nine and changing the type of interval accordingly, you can invert intervals like a pro!

Extended Intervals

The largest interval you've learned about so far is the octave. Intervals are a basic ingredient in chords. Most traditional chords don't deal with notes over the octave, or at least they don't differentiate between them. Modern chords, especially jazz chords, deal with extended intervals—intervals that are larger than the octave. **FIGURE 13-11** shows a two-octave scale showing the extended intervals.

FIGURE 13-11 Extended Intervals

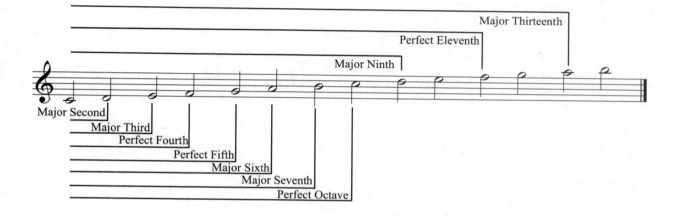

You will notice that above the eighth note (the octave), only the ninth, eleventh, and thirteenth are named. The tenth, twelfth, and fourteenth are left blank. This is one of those things that has evolved in music over a long time. The basic reason is that the excluded notes (eighth, tenth, and twelfth) make up the basic ingredients of chords, also called triads. You know that roots, thirds, and fifths don't sound all that different regardless of what octave they are in. Because of this, they are considered roots, thirds, and fifths no matter where they are in the musical spectrum. The other notes— the ninth, eleventh, and thirteenth—do sound quite different from their lower counterparts. Above the octave, the intervals read like this:

- A second up the octave becomes a ninth
- A fourth up the octave becomes an eleventh
- A sixth up the octave becomes a thirteenth

The second and ninth are differentiated because they sound very different from each other. A second can be dissonant and crunchy, while a ninth can be a beautiful sonorous sound. Jazz chords make use of these higher extensions very frequently. More on this in Chapter 20.

Interval Quiz

Just for fun, **FIGURE 13-12** is an interval quiz. Do this in pencil, in case you make a mistake. Good luck! The answer to this is in Appendix C.

FIGURE 13-12 Interval Quiz

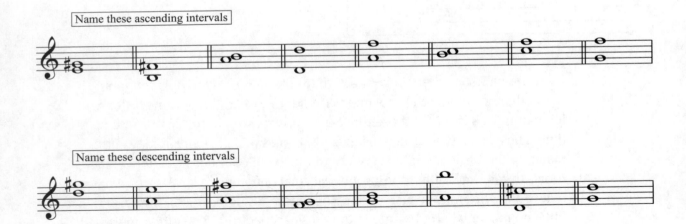

Chapter 14

Vertical Thinking: Triads, Chords, Arpeggios, and Seventh Chords

It's time to think big. Scales and intervals combine to form chords, which are the foundation of our system of harmony. Chords come in various forms and types but are all based on the same basic principles. If you understand how to build a simple major scale, then you can understand a great deal about chords.

Chord Origins

Those of you who play harmonic instruments (piano, guitar) deal with chords on a daily basis. Those of you who play single-note instruments may not have much familiarity with chords because you can't play them on your instruments. Chords are an essential part of music, and whether or not you can play them on your instrument, you will need to understand them. Even if you can't physically play chords, their effects can be felt in your music as well.

What is a chord? A chord is best described as a grouping of three or more notes played simultaneously. The minimum number of notes you need for a chord is three, but there can also be many more than three. Pianists often play more than three notes in chords.

E ALERT!

A chord is at least three notes—not just three keys on the piano. It takes three separate note names to form a chord. You can freely duplicate or spread those notes around. Don't let the number of notes on the page scare you; look for the individual pitches.

Major and Minor Triads

Simple chords are also called triads. Triads take their prefix from tri, or three. A triad is a three-note chord, built on intervals of thirds. Chord is the more general name for notes played together; triads are a specific kind of chord. Triads are always just a root, a third, and a fifth played together. As you learned in Chapters 11 and 12, you can combine the first, third, and fifth notes of both the major and the minor scales to form major and minor triads (see **FIGURE 14-1**).

FIGURE 14-1
Major and Minor
Triads

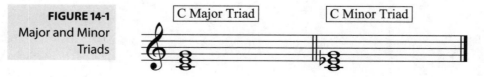

C Major Triad   C Minor Triad

To spell any major and minor chord, you select the first, third, and fifth notes of any major or minor scale. These are the major and minor triads. This is certainly one way to spell chords. Unfortunately, using this method, you can only spell major and minor triads—other triads exist besides major and minor.

Since triads are always built with thirds, on a music staff they always come out looking like the ones shown in **FIGURE 14-2**. No matter what the triad is, it's always going to be on lines or spaces! This makes the task of naming triads easier.

FIGURE 14-2 Triads on Lines and Spaces

Barring the sharps and flats, triads will always be one of these sets of notes:

- A C E
- B D F
- C E G
- D F A
- E G B
- F A C
- G B D

Those are all the possible combinations of triads in the musical alphabet. That's it! Of course, certain notes will have sharps and others will have flats, but all triads will adhere to those groupings. There are only seven, and many of them share two notes together. For example, C E G (C Major) and A C E (A Minor) both include C and E. This is a huge step in speeding up your understanding of triads.

The Difference Between a Triad and a Chord

A triad is the simplest way to express harmony. Triads always appear in order: root, third, and fifth. Triads are "perfect" examples of chords, laid out in simple form. From a triad, you learn what notes appear in chords. Rarely do you see triads in real music. As soon as composers start playing with the order of notes, doubling notes or spreading the notes across the staff, you are dealing with chords. The term chord is used for harmonies of more than three notes, so the distinction is important. Instead of seeing stock triads, you're more apt to see something like **FIGURE 14-3**.

FIGURE 14-3 Triads to Chords

TRACK 56

C Triad - Closed Position.

Both Contain C E G.
The Voicing On The Right Simply
Reorders The Pitches And Doubles
C and G.
Both Are Considered C Chords.

C Major Chord.

Look at the Intervals

Some of the knowledge of intervals you gained from the last chapter can also be applied to chords. To learn major and minor scales, you examined the intervals between the notes and came up with easy-to-learn patterns. By now, **WWHWWWH** is a familiar and easy way to spell a major scale because the pattern of intervals never changes. This pattern thinking does not just apply to scales—chords utilize the same sort of repeating interval patterns. The good news is that chords are usually only three notes, so you're not going to have to learn long interval patterns.

Major Triad Intervals

The C major triad contains the notes C E G. As long as those notes appear together, regardless of the order, it is a C major chord. Let's look at how this triad is constructed in **FIGURE 14-4**.

FIGURE 14-4 Major Triad Intervals

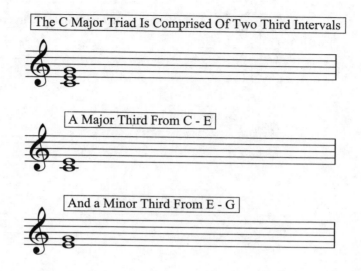

The C Major Triad Is Comprised Of Two Third Intervals

A Major Third From C - E

And a Minor Third From E - G

As mentioned, a triad is a three-note chord built on third intervals. Between the C and E is a major third. Between the E and G is a minor third. Major third, minor third is the distinctive pattern of a major triad. No other triad or chord has that formula exactly the same way. If you were to apply this to any root, you could spell the notes in any major chord.

Minor Triad Intervals

The C minor triad contains the notes C E♭ G (see **FIGURE 14-5**). Between the C and the E♭ is a minor third. Between the E♭ and the G is a major third. The pattern for a minor triad is minor third, major third. This is the reverse of the major triad formula. It's also easy to remember! Minor triads have a minor third first. Major triads have a major third first. They are both followed by the opposite third interval.

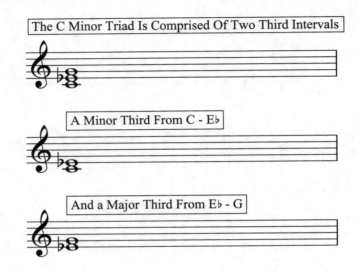

FIGURE 14-5 Minor Triad Intervals

The C Minor Triad Is Comprised Of Two Third Intervals

A Minor Third From C - E♭

And a Major Third From E♭ - G

Diminished and Augmented Chords

In music, there are four basic triads. No matter what style of music you play, everything starts with these four triads: major triad, minor triad, diminished triad, or augmented triad. From these four basic triads, we form the basic understanding of harmony. Composers build upon the triads for jazz chords and other harmonies.

For major and minor triads, you started with either the major or minor scale and selected the first, third, and fifth notes to make the respective triads. In the case of diminished and augmented, there are no scales to look at to easily form these triads. These triads are formed entirely on intervals or in relation to other triads you already know.

FIGURE 14-6 shows a C diminished triad.

FIGURE 14-6 Diminished Triad

TRACK 57

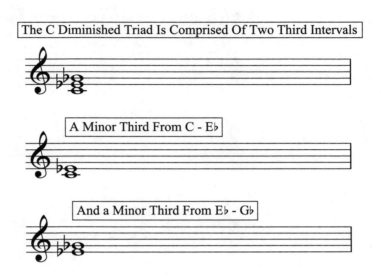

The C Diminished Triad Is Comprised Of Two Third Intervals

A Minor Third From C - E♭

And a Minor Third From E♭ - G♭

Since all triads are some combination of thirds, the diminished triad is no exception. As you'll remember, major and minor triads contained one of each kind of third: one major third and one minor third. A diminished triad contains two minor thirds, a minor third between C and E♭ and another minor third between E♭ and G♭. Diminished triads have a unique and distinctive sound to them. Many find them puzzling and tense-sounding. The movies use diminished chords in very suspenseful moments. Remember the old black-and-white movie where the girl is tied to the tracks and the train creeps closer? That's a diminished chord you'll hear accompanying it. Simply place two minor thirds together and you get an instant diminished triad.

At this point, we're running out of thirds to combine. The only thing left to do is stick two major thirds together. If you did, you'd get **FIGURE 14-7**. An augmented triad is the result of stacking two major thirds together. Augmented triads have a very open and dreamy sound.

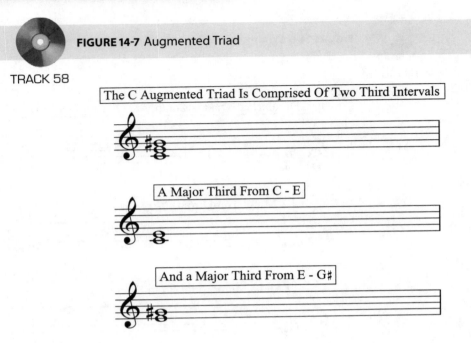

TRACK 58

FIGURE 14-7 Augmented Triad

The C Augmented Triad Is Comprised Of Two Third Intervals

A Major Third From C - E

And a Major Third From E - G♯

Relating Triads to Major

You now know four triads: major, minor, augmented, and diminished. Each has its own sound and distinctive blueprint. Here is another way to look at triads that might make it a little easier for you. The world of music theory has always revolved around major scales and major harmonies. They are so commonly used that people often relate everything else to major because it's so clear in their minds. You can do the same thing for triads. If you start from the basic C major triad, you can see the distinctions:

- To go from a major triad to a minor triad, lower the third note of the major triad (see **FIGURE 14-8**).
- To go from a major triad to a diminished triad, lower the third and the fifth notes of the major triad (see **FIGURE 14-9**).
- To go from a major triad to an augmented triad, raise the fifth note of the major triad (see **FIGURE 14-10**).

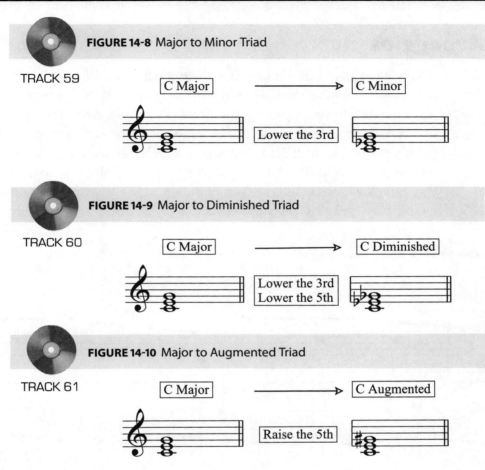

TRACK 59

FIGURE 14-8 Major to Minor Triad

TRACK 60

FIGURE 14-9 Major to Diminished Triad

TRACK 61

FIGURE 14-10 Major to Augmented Triad

While they are aware of the intervalic nature of chords, most musicians relate them either to scales or to adaptations of other familiar chords. As you use chords frequently, you'll memorize them. **FIGURE 14-11** shows a recap of all the triads, starting with the root of C.

FIGURE 14-11 Triad Recap

Arpeggios

If you can't play chords on your instrument, you aren't left out of this discussion. Chords and triads are notes that are played together on harmonic instruments. However, playing the notes of a triad or chord one at a time or "broken up" is called playing an arpeggio. The word arpeggio literally means "to break" in Italian. In tonal music, harmonies and melodies are formed out of scales and triads. Even if you play a single-note instrument, you can play harmonies based on chords; you just have to do it one note at a time, via arpeggios (see **FIGURE 14-12**).

FIGURE 14-12 Triads into Arpeggios

TRACK 62

You can play an arpeggio of any chord. Arpeggio playing is a fixture of all music on all instruments, regardless of how many notes they can play at one time. Arpeggios are the same notes as chords, played one at a time. Composers use arpeggios to spell out harmony for instruments that can't play more than one note at a time. Look at the example from the well-known Mozart Clarinet Concerto in A (K. 622) in **FIGURE 14-13**.

FIGURE 14-13 Mozart Clarinet Arpeggios

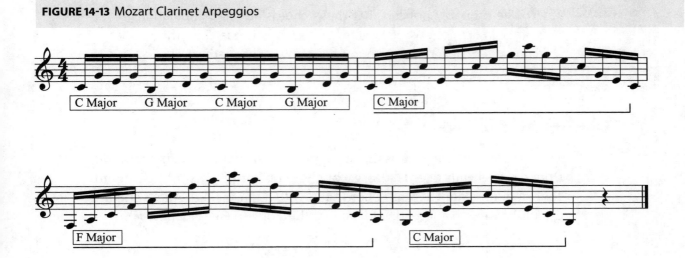

Below the music you see the bracketed sections where chords are outlined via arpeggios. If you play a single-note instrument, make sure to play through all of the chords and triads as arpeggios—you're going to encounter them in your instrumental music often.

Seventh Chords

The next step up on the evolutionary musical ladder is seventh chords. You already know that a triad is composed of two third intervals put together. Add one more third interval on the top of the basic triads to form seventh chords. G7 chords, if you're familiar with them, are one example of a seventh chord.

There are four basic triads: major, minor, diminished, and augmented. There are two types of thirds, major and minor. If you combine the triads with the additional third intervals, you get eight more chords. This chapter covers the common and useful ones. For now, we are going to look at dominant seventh, major seventh, minor seventh, and diminished seventh. There are four more seventh chords, included in Appendix A.

You've probably noticed that these chords are all combinations of thirds. In fact, our whole system of harmony is based on thirds. The correct term is tertiary harmony, harmony based on thirds.

Dominant Seventh

The dominant seventh is the most common seventh chord in the world. Dominant seventh chords also go by the moniker of 7, as in a G7 chord. To form a dominant seventh chord, start with a major triad. After you have established the major triad, add a minor third on top (see **FIGURE 14-14**).

FIGURE 14-14 Dominant Seventh Chord

TRACK 63

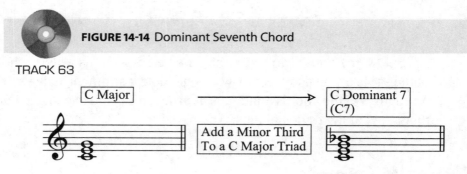

The added B♭ forms a minor seventh interval, measuring from the root of C. So you could also say that a dominant seventh is a major triad with an added minor seventh. Either way you think about it, you come to the same conclusion. This is a very useful chord in all styles and forms of music. The term dominant will become much clearer in Chapter 15 when we discuss scale harmony. This is one important chord!

Major Seventh

Start with another major triad, but this time add a major third on top. The result is the major seventh chord (see **FIGURE 14-15**).

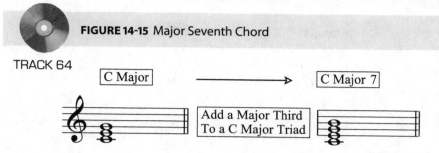

FIGURE 14-15 Major Seventh Chord

TRACK 64

The major seventh chord is a beautiful chord, which instantly sounds "jazzy." It's a favorite among composers for its bright, warm sound. You'll see this more in modern music than in classical music, although it is in some classical music, even as far back as J.S. Bach. The interval between the root C and the seventh B is a major seventh interval. So, if you take a major triad and add a major seventh interval, you form a major seventh chord.

Minor Seventh

How could we leave out minor chords? Let's start with a minor triad and add a minor third on top of that (see **FIGURE 14-16**).

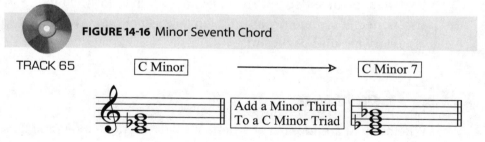

FIGURE 14-16 Minor Seventh Chord

TRACK 65

This is a great sounding chord which is used often. Look at the interval between the C and B♭—you'll see another minor seventh. A minor seventh chord is composed of a minor triad with a minor seventh interval added.

Diminished Seventh

Diminished seventh chords are an interesting case. Very rarely do you see a straight diminished triad. More often than not you'll come across the diminished seventh chord, mainly because it sounds better for the purpose. Start with a diminished triad and add another minor third interval. The result is **FIGURE 14-17**.

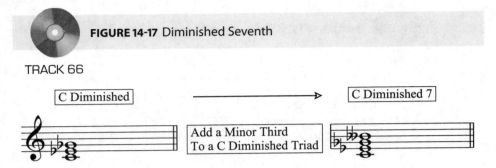

FIGURE 14-17 Diminished Seventh

TRACK 66

The diminished seventh is called a fully diminished seventh chord because another type of diminished seventh chord exists, called the half diminished seventh chord. It's important to describe the chord properly, as musicians are aware of the other type of diminished seventh chord.

The interval between the C and the B♭♭ is a diminished seventh interval. This is also a great time to point out the use of the double flat. B♭♭ really sounds like an A, but to keep the convention of using thirds, a third from G♭ has to be the letter B of some sort.

A diminished chord is formed from a diminished triad with a diminished seventh interval added on. The chord has a very cool and unique sound. It's also perfectly symmetric, as all the intervals are minor thirds—it spells the same forward and backward.

Triad Inversion

Whether you are looking at a perfect triad or a huge ten-note piano chord, the lowest note in the chord is very important. If the lowest note in the chord is the same note as the root of the chord, then that chord is said to be in root position. A root position chord is the most common chord that you will see. Many guitar players go their whole life without playing any chords but root position chords. All of the triads in this chapter have appeared in root position.

Whenever another note of the chord appears as the lowest sounding note, it's called a chord inversion. For simple triads, there are two possible inversions: first inversion and second inversion. There is also a third possible inversion for seventh chords.

First Inversion

A first inversion triad is any chord that has the third of the chord as the lowest note (see **FIGURE 14-18**). The appearance of the rest of the chord makes no difference. The key ingredients are that all the notes of the C major triad are there (C E G) and that the lowest sounding note is an E, which is the third of the chord. This makes this a first inversion C major chord.

In **FIGURE 14-18**, you see that the chord has been named two ways. The first way is the more traditional classical theory method of naming a first inversion triad. The small 6 denotes that this is in first inversion. Its origin comes from the fact that there is now a sixth interval between the lowest part of the chord and the highest. It is a term only used in classical music. The modern way to describe this chord is C/E. C/E indicates that it's a C major chord with an E as its lowest note. The formula is triad/bass note. You'll see this method of naming chords and chord inversions used commonly today.

FIGURE 14-18 First Inversion

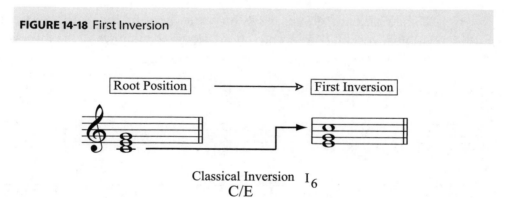

Second Inversion

Since the first inversion involved placing the third in the bass, the smart money says that the second inversion places the fifth of the chord in the bass. If you thought this, you are correct! **FIGURE 14-19** shows a second inversion C major triad.

FIGURE 14-19 Second Inversion

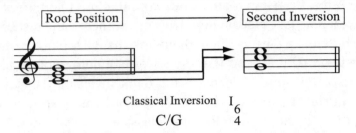

Again, it does not matter how the rest of the chord looks. For this to be a second inversion triad, the fifth of the chord must be the lowest sounding note. Classical theory designates this as a 6/4 triad, named because the intervals above the bass are a sixth and a fourth, respectively. Modern chord notation uses the symbol C/G (C major chord, G bass note).

Seventh Chord Inversions

Since seventh chords have an extra note in them, there is a third possible inversion of a seventh chord. **FIGURE 14-20** shows all the inversions of a dominant seventh chord in a musical example.

FIGURE 14-20 Seventh Chord Inversions

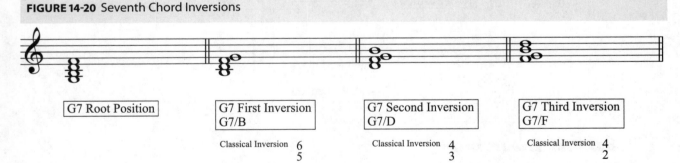

In this example we have shown not only the inverted triads, but the classical and modern way of writing inversions. Notice that when you deal with seventh chords, the classical style of "6" and "6/4" used for inversions change for the seventh chords. This is because 6 and 6/4 refer to interval patterns in the chords. Since seventh chords form new interval patterns, their corresponding numbers change based on the new intervals between the notes. Seventh chords employ abbreviated interval pattern numbers (e.g., 4/3 or 4/2) below the chords.

The numerical inversion symbols are complex. They're important to understand but their practice is beyond the scope of this text. Memorizing them will come in handy if you study music theory in an academic setting. If not, don't worry too much; the modern symbol of letter/letter is more common now than the academic approach.

Chords Written as Symbols

Chords don't always appear in written music as stacks of notes. Very often, especially in jazz and show music, you'll find chords written out as symbols of text. The player is responsible for knowing how to play that chord in a comfortable way on her instrument. Over the years, several conventions for writing out chords have been used and, unfortunately, no one standard exists. Here are the symbols you're most likely to see:

- For major chords: C, Cmaj, CM, C△
- For minor chords: Cmin, Cm, C-
- For diminished chords: C°, C dim.
- For augmented chords: C+, C aug.
- For dominant seventh chords: C7
- For major seventh chords: Cmaj7, CM7, C△7
- For minor seventh chords: Cmin7, Cm7, C-7
- For diminished seventh chords: Cdim7, C°7
- For chord inversions (which are always handled the same way, regardless of the kind of triad they are): C/E = Name of the triad/ bass note

You won't see the classical style of chord inversions in the modern style of writing chord inversions.

Chapter 15
Basic Harmony 101

Harmony is a multifaceted term in music. Harmony deals with the ability of notes to sound together in a pleasing fashion. Studying harmony will show you the connection between scales, chords, and melody. Harmony is one of the most important aspects of music theory to learn.

What Is Harmony?

What exactly is harmony and why is it important? Let's start by looking at a few possible definitions of what harmony is.

- Harmony is a pleasing combination of musical sounds.
- Harmony is any combination of notes that are sung or played at the same time.
- Harmony is the study of the way in which musical chords are constructed and how they function in relation to one another.

No matter how you define harmony, it's a topic you're going to want to learn a great deal about. The study of what notes sound good when played together and what notes do not enables you to understand music on a deeper level.

Harmony deals with notes that sound together. This can be two notes together in a counterpoint or a piece for full symphony orchestra. However, for the purposes of this book and learning to read music, you'll learn about harmony in relation to chords and chord progressions. Chords are more than just stacks of intervals. Chords have their origins in scales and melodies. Looking at music history can clarify some of the elements about chords and their relationship to scales.

ALERT!

Remember that theory is backward-looking. The whole genre of music theory looks back on music that has already been composed and tries to explain what it sees. It does not dictate what can be. Composers typically learn their craft by studying the works of the masters who came before them and continuing the evolution forward. You can't blame them for trying to figure out what made Beethoven so wonderful, can you?

Some of the earliest forms of music were vocal-oriented. A great deal of music was sacred and revolved around the church. Vocal music began as just one single melody, known as monophony or a monophonic melody. In time, additional melodies were added, called polyphony. The melodies moved in a left-to-right fashion across the page. Of course, the notes in all of the melodies had to complement each other. You can't just sing anything! Certain notes sound good together and others do not. Composers were able to play/hear/imagine what intervals sounded good together. As music evolved, more melodies were played at once, and more vocal parts were added.

FIGURE 15-1 is an example of a four-part chorale by J.S. Bach, who pretty much perfected the genre of four-part writing. What you see here is four separate vocal melodies to be performed by four separate singers. Each has his or her own melody to sing. Here is where the vertical component comes into play. Look at the first note in the piece. All those notes sound at exactly the same time. They form a chord—a G major chord, to be exact! Vertical thinking shows that even though there are four separate melodies, when you look at how the notes from all of the parts "stack up," you'll start to see that chords appear. It makes sense—how else would four people be able to sing together if there weren't some sort of system in place? Choosing random notes on a piano to play together won't result in a pleasant sound— there has to be a system and an order.

FIGURE 15-1 Bach Four-Part Chorale

BWV 175

J.S. Bach

Consonance vs. Dissonance

As harmony developed, it did so one voice at a time. When the second voice was added, certain musical intervals were considered consonant and could be sounded together, while other intervals were dissonant and were avoided. Consonant intervals include thirds, fourths, fifths, sixths, and octaves. Dissonant intervals include seconds, tritones, and sevenths. When the third and fourth voices of polyphony were added, the consonances stacked up as chords; this is how music and harmony came to be.

FACT

Over the course of music history, what is considered consonant and dissonant has changed. At first, perfect fourths were considered a dissonance, but today they are more common.

Basic Scale Harmony

Scales are very important. This cannot be overstated. They are nothing short of musical DNA—an essential building block. Let's revisit the C major triad (see **FIGURE 15-2**).

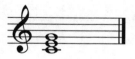

FIGURE 15-2 C Major Triad

This triad can be constructed a few different ways. One of the ways is to take the first, third, and fifth notes of the C major scale and stack them together. By doing this, you are able to build a quick C major triad. This trick works in every major and minor scale, so in theory you could build any major or minor chord you need to. Since chords are built from third intervals, it would make sense that you could do more than just stack the first, third, and fifth notes together. There are a whole bunch of possible third combinations in a scale. What would happen if you stacked these different combinations? You'd get a whole bunch of chords.

You are going to learn how to make triads from every note in a C major scale. To do this, let's start out with a C major scale (**FIGURE 15-3**). Now, let's place third intervals above each note in the scale. The result looks like **FIGURE 15-4**. The final step is to add another third and make these into full triads (see **FIGURE 15-5**). Listen to the recorded example of this. What you've just done is create all of the harmonies in the key of C major by creating triads off of each note.

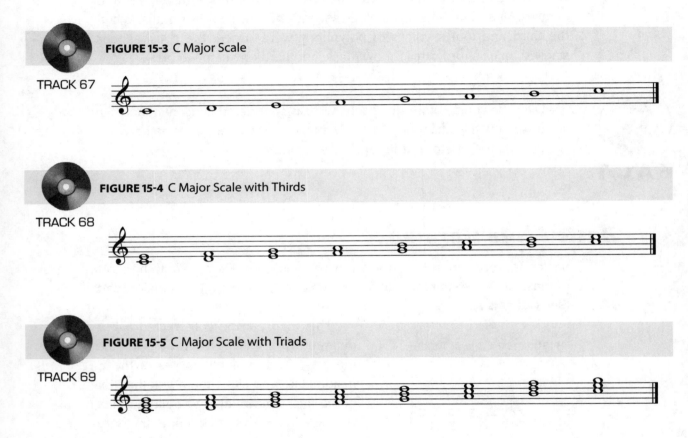

FIGURE 15-3 C Major Scale

TRACK 67

FIGURE 15-4 C Major Scale with Thirds

TRACK 68

FIGURE 15-5 C Major Scale with Triads

TRACK 69

Don't downplay the significance of this. You've just learned the basis for understanding harmony and chord progressions. Contained within those triads are seven different chords and endless possibilities for creating music. When you create triads from a scale and only use those notes to do so, you use a technique called diatonic harmony. Diatonic means using the notes from only one scale/key to make chords.

Diatonic Chords

In the last section, you took a C major scale and added triads to each note in the scale, creating seven diatonic triads in that key. Let's look at exactly what chords are created from making these triads.

You can see from the example in **FIGURE 15-6** that not only are three major chords created, but three minor chords and one diminished chord are also formed. Who knew that they were all hiding inside the simple C major scale?

FIGURE 15-6 C Major Triads Named

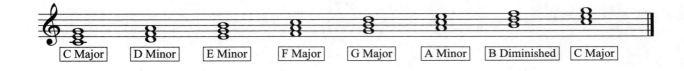

| C Major | D Minor | E Minor | F Major | G Major | A Minor | B Diminished | C Major |

The Order of Triads

The order of triads in the scale is important. In a major scale/key, the triads always progress in this order: major, minor, minor, major, major, minor, and diminished. Memorize this; it's going to serve you quite well in the future.

And the best part is that what you've just done in the key of C major holds true in every major key. Since all major scales are constructed in the exact same fashion, with the exact same intervals, when you stack triads in any major scale you always get the same order of triads/chords. This is a huge time saver! The only thing that changes are the names of the notes themselves, as no two keys have the exact same pitches. The chords and their order will always be the same. **FIGURE 15-7** gives an example in the key of C major, E♭ major, and B major to show you that no matter what the scale is, the same order of triads always exists.

FIGURE 15-7 Triads in Other Keys

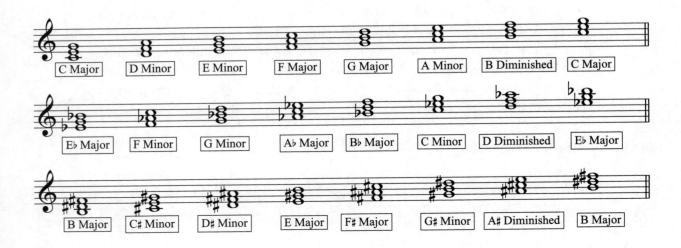

Notice that the notes in the scales are in different keys, but the order of chords (major, minor, minor, major, major, minor, and diminished) stays the same. This holds true for every major scale/key.

Roman Numerals

To music theorists, there isn't any real difference between any major key. Unless you possess the ability of "perfect pitch," where you can name a note just listening to it, you won't be able to hear a difference between C major and D major scales. Since there is such equality in the keys, music theory has a system of naming chords relative to what note of the scale they are built from. If you were to number the notes of the C major scale, you'd get **FIGURE 15-8**.

FIGURE 15-8 C Major Scale Numbered

As triads are built off of the notes, they can now be referred to by number. For example, a one chord in the key of C major is the chord built off of the first note in the scale, which is C major. Since every major scale starts with a major triad, you could say that the one chord in any major key was major. Do this for all of the triads and the result is the chart in **FIGURE 15-9**.

FIGURE 15-9 C Major Triads Numbered

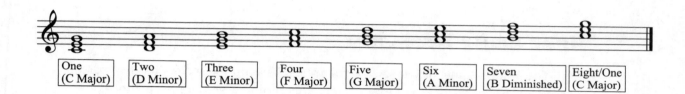

| One
(C Major) | Two
(D Minor) | Three
(E Minor) | Four
(F Major) | Five
(G Major) | Six
(A Minor) | Seven
(B Diminished) | Eight/One
(C Major) |

The only limitation with using numbers this way is that there is no way to convey whether that chord is major or minor simply by using the number 1, 2, or 3. Musicians use Roman numerals instead of Arabic numbers for this very reason. You may remember from math class that Roman numerals have lowercase equivalents. By using uppercase Roman numerals for major chords and lowercase Roman numerals for minor chords, musicians have a system that makes sense in every key and conveys a lot of information about a chord. **FIGURE 15-10** shows the harmonized C major scale with all of the corresponding Roman numerals. You'll also notice that the diminished chord is denoted by a lowercase Roman numeral and a small degree sign next to it. That's the standard way to indicate diminished chords.

FIGURE 15-10 C Major Triads with Roman Numerals

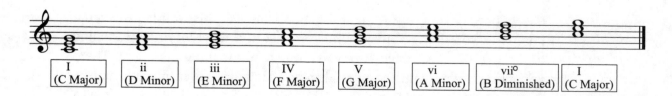

| I
(C Major) | ii
(D Minor) | iii
(E Minor) | IV
(F Major) | V
(G Major) | vi
(A Minor) | vii°
(B Diminished) | I
(C Major) |

Minor Scale Harmony

The minor scale has a few peculiarities. The minor scale has the exact same notes as the major scale and accordingly should have the exact same resulting chords, just in a different order, but the minor scale has some quirks when it comes to harmony. You may recall from Chapter 12 the harmonic minor scale, which was a minor scale with a raised seventh tone. The harmonic minor scale exists solely to correct the harmony of the minor scale and make it more suitable. Let's look at a "normal" minor scale harmonized with triads to see what we get (see **FIGURE 15-11**).

FIGURE 15-11 A Minor Scale Harmonized

TRACK 70

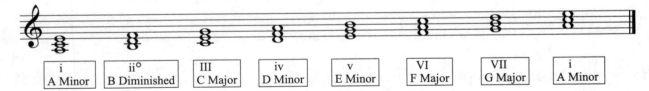

i A Minor	ii° B Diminished	III C Major	iv D Minor	v E Minor	VI F Major	VII G Major	i A Minor

By harmonizing the A natural minor scale like this, you get the same chords as you did in C major; they are just in a different order. Listening to the CD track for **FIGURE 15-11**, you won't hear anything dissonant. There is nothing wrong with the natural minor scale. However, in tonal music, that minor scale is not harmonized, because it's lacking what is known as a proper dominant chord.

The Dominant Chord

Dominant chords are the single most critical element of harmony to understand. The fifth chord, or V as it's written in a Roman numeral, is an unbelievably important chord. The chord built on the fifth note of a scale is commonly referred to as the dominant chord, because it has such a strong pull to it. When you are in a key and you come to the V chord, it has a tremendously unresolved feeling to it. Listen to the example in **FIGURE 15-12**.

FIGURE 15-12 Example of a Dominant Chord

TRACK 71

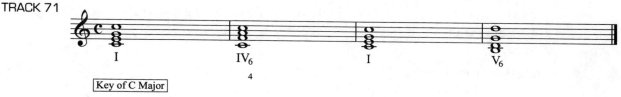

This example ends on the V chord in the key of C major, the G major chord. It's hard to explain why it feels like this musical example isn't finished. There is just something to the V chord that makes it want to be resolved. This "pull" is what makes tonal music what it is. Tonal music is defined as the relationship of the dominant chord to the tonic chord. The tonic chord is the I, or one, chord in the key—the chord that the scale is built on. In the key of C major, the tonic chord is C major. Let's complete the last example and resolve that pesky dominant chord (see **FIGURE 15-13**).

FIGURE 15-13 Dominant Chord Resolving

TRACK 72

Something about the sounds of those chords resolving the way they do is very pleasing. This push and pull is what makes tonal music what it is.

Dominant Chords in the Major Scale

In the major scale, the chord built on the fifth note is a major chord. In every major scale, the dominant chord V is always major. The fact that this chord is major is what gives it the unbelievable pull back to the tonic I chord. The reason that the V chord pulls so hard to the I chord is because the V chord contains the seventh note of the scale in the chord. The seventh tone, or leading tone as it's also called, is a superstrong tone that pulls up like a magnet to the eighth tone of the scale. Look at and listen to the example in **FIGURE 15-14**.

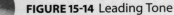

FIGURE 15-14 Leading Tone

TRACK 73

Leading Tone

Stopping at the leading tone is almost criminal. It's quite amazing what that sounds like. It's also equally amazing that words can't describe it. In the case of the C major scale, the V chord is G major, which contains the leading tone (B) in the chord. Every major scale automatically has this built into it. The minor scale by default does not.

Dominants in a Minor Scale

When you harmonize the minor scale, you get a pattern of chords. Let's use C minor this time to see the harmonized parallels between C major (see **FIGURE 15-15**).

FIGURE 15-15 C Minor Scale Harmonized

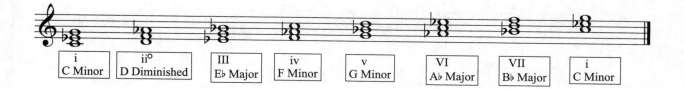

You learned in the last section that a dominant chord needs to be built on the fifth note of the scale and the chord needs to be major. Looking at this C minor scale, you see that the V chord is G minor. No good. G minor will not pull as a dominant chord should because the chord and the minor scale are both missing the leading tone. Remember the harmonic minor scale? It is a natural minor scale with a raised seventh note, giving it a leading tone. The result of adding the leading tone, or a B♮ in this case, is that it affects a few of the chords. You guessed it. The dominant chord now becomes major. Now there is a dominant V chord in a minor key. **FIGURE 15-16** shows what the harmonized harmonic minor scale looks like.

FIGURE 15-16 Harmonic Minor Scale Harmonized

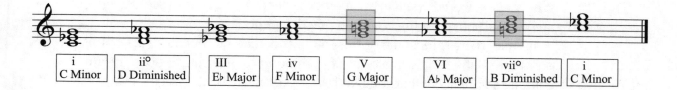

Because the dominant chord now has the pull it needs, the minor key now sounds fuller and more complete. Listen to the example in **FIGURE 15-17** and hear for yourself. Without the change of the leading tone and the resulting dominant V chord, the minor key wouldn't "work" nearly as effectively.

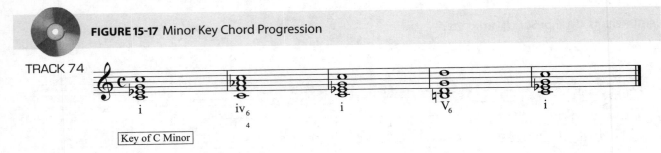

FIGURE 15-17 Minor Key Chord Progression

TRACK 74

Key of C Minor

The other thing you'll notice is that the seventh chord, which used to be B♭ major, is now B diminished. You'll also notice that in the III chord, the B remains flat. That's covered in greater detail in Chapter 16 on chord progressions. For now, just be aware that when you change any single note of any scale, a few chords are affected.

Minor/Dominant Conventions

The dominant chord is so important that even though it isn't naturally present in a stock minor scale, musicians put it there anyway. The scale is altered from how it appears normally just to preserve the relationship between the dominant and the tonic. This is not something that is done only some of the time. In tonal music, the minor scale is almost always altered this way. Without the dominant chord pull, it just wouldn't sound the same. The III chord remains unaltered because the result of changing the seventh scale degree would result in an augmented chord on the third scale degree, an unusual sound for the common practice period.

While there are some forms of music that do not adhere to this convention, the largest majority of common practice music does. In any case, it's so prevalent that you need to be very aware of it. If you ever want to write music, learning to control these basic sounds is your most important lesson. This can't be stressed enough. Figure out V and I chords and you will understand tonal music—everything else revolves around this.

There is plenty of music that does not use a dominant V chord. To prove a point of how important the dominant is, music that does not employ a raised seventh/dominant V chord has a completely different musical sound, one that is identified by its lack of a dominant chord. For example, Renaissance music often does not employ this technique—hence its unique sound.

Chapter 16
Basic Major Scale Chord Progressions

Now you understand how scales are used to build up chords and create basic harmony. That information leads to learning about all the chords that are available in any key. Knowing what chords are available is useful to understanding which chords can be used in a particular key and can help you recognize which ones you'll encounter most often when reading music. Understanding how chords move, group, and interact is the study of chord progressions.

Correlating Melody and Harmony

In the last few chapters, you have built up a firm knowledge of scales, intervals, and chords that help you understand how music is put together. The manner in which chords are grouped together, or chord progressions as they are more commonly called, is the study of how composers and musicians utilize harmony. This is one of the most pivotal steps in understanding how music is written. Before you can analyze repeating chord structures, you need to understand the relationship between chords and melody.

How do melody and harmony relate to each other? The relationship between melody and harmony can dictate the kinds of chords used in a piece. One of the hardest questions to ask is "Which came first: melody or harmony?" This is akin to the-chicken-or-the-egg question! It is known that in music history, melody came first and chords grew from the vertical collisions of melodies. That was then, this is now. Now, chords are entities in themselves.

At the minimum, a chord must contain three separate notes. It can contain many more, but for it to be considered a "chord," the minimum is three notes.

A chord is a grouping of notes that are played together. And melodies are groupings of notes that are played one after another. Since both chords and melodies deal with notes, it makes sense to think there must be a correlation in how they are used—and there is.

Chords as Supports

Chords can play a supportive role. They help hold up the melodies over them. In the most basic sense, a melody is made up from notes in a chord or chords. You have learned about the concept of dissonance versus consonance. Chords and melodies are no different. Here is a rule to get you started: When a chord is sounding, the melody that is played simultaneously should be consonant to the chord. It makes perfect sense. Chords typically accompany melodies, so it makes sense that they are related. Let's look at a popular song and see how the melody and harmony are related. **FIGURE 16-1** is a short excerpt from the Christmas classic "Silent Night."

FIGURE 16-1 "Silent Night" Analysis

TRACK 75

There are three main elements here to look at. The first is the melody line. Below that are the chords that support the melody, written in standard notation. To keep it simple, this version uses simple triads. Above the melody are the shorthand symbols for the chords. Let's look at each section of music, chord by chord, to see how the melody and the harmony interact.

"Silent Night" Breakdown

Whenever a particular chord is ringing, all of the melodic notes are interacting with the chord in some way. But how do the chords and the melodies relate? Looking at the key signature of **FIGURE 16-1** and the existence of G major chords, you can decide that this melody is in the key of G major. The first excerpt (**FIGURE 16-2**) is the first two measures.

FIGURE 16-2 First Two Measures, "Silent Night"

There is a G major chord (G B D) ringing in the harmony. While that chord is ringing, the melody should be related to the chords. You can see in the melody some numbers below the melody line in Figure 16-2. These name the intervals of the melody against the G chord. The melody in this section is composed of three main tones: D, E, and B. Both the D and B are tones from the G major chord and the E, while not in the chord, is still a consonant tone to the chord. It also does not sound for very long, so even if it was a slight dissonance, it is resolved quickly. Notes that are not in the chords are aptly called non-chord tones. The note E in Figure 16.2 is an example of a non-chord tone. Tonal music can be broken up into two categories: chord tones and non-chord tones. In "Silent Night," both exist. The important thing is that in the first two measures, the notes in the melody are almost all found in the chord that accompanies it.

The last two measures (**FIGURE 16-3**) of this piece have two chords, D major and G major. These measures are even simpler: The notes in the melody come directly from the chords. When the D major chord is ringing, the melody is composed of A and F$\sharp$, the fifth and third of the D chord. In the last measure, a G major chord accompanies a G and D melody, the root and fifth of the G major chord.

FIGURE 16-3 Last Two Measures, "Silent Night"

Harmonic Breakdown and Conclusions

In this short four-measure excerpt there are two chords, G major and D major. You know this piece is in the key of G major because it has a one-sharp key signature and G major chords accompanying.

The harmony chosen for this piece is G and D major chords, or I and V if we were using Roman numerals. In the last chapter, you learned that the two most important chords in any key are the I and the V chords. Not surprisingly, that's exactly what you find in this excerpt. One of the things that makes "Silent Night" such a good song to start with when you're learning to look at harmony and melody is that the melody is so closely taken from the chords. Or is it the other way around . . . ?

Chicken or Egg?

So it's not too difficult to break down a simple melody into its parts and see the relationship of the melody to the harmony. But which came first? Was the harmony in place first and the composer picked a melody that fit with those chords? Or did the melody come first and the harmony come after? There's no way to know for sure, since the composer is no longer around to tell us. The smart money says that the melody came first and chords were chosen that "worked" with the particular melody. Experienced musicians and composers can conceive of harmony and melody at the same time.

This is something that can be difficult to grasp as we cover chord progressions separately from melodies. Just remember that if a melody comes first, it affects which chords will be used. If the chords come first, the melody will be affected. You have to look at both sides of this coin to fully understand its meaning.

Basics of Chord Progressions

Different composers wrote in different ways, yet looking at a cross-section of composers across the generations reveals the same chords and progressions. Learning about standard chord progressions will help you understand how scales are harmonized and why composers choose the progressions they do.

Diatonic

In Chapter 15, you saw how simple major and minor scales could be harmonized with triads. The result was seven chords for the major scales and seven chords for the minor scales. Harmonizing triads based on a straight major or minor scale creates diatonic harmony, which literally means "from the key." When musicians talk about chord progressions in Roman numerals, they are assumed to be diatonic chords from one single scale.

The Importance of the Tonic and Dominant

The basis of tonal harmony and chord progressions is the relationship of two chords: tonic (the I chord) and dominant (the V chord). While it's hard to make sweeping generalizations about music in any sense, this much is certain: You're going to find more tonic and dominant chords in tonal music than almost any other chords. In fact, if you want to be sure what key you are in, searching for the ubiquitous I and V chords will always give you a definite answer.

The Mighty V7 Chord

In Chapter 14 you learned how to harmonize all of the triads with the additional sevenths, making them seventh chords. Most traditional music theory doesn't deal with seventh chords alone. The predominant chord is the simple three-note triad. The only notable exception is the dominant, or V, chord. In traditional music, the dominant chord often appears as a seventh chord. The reason for this is pretty interesting.

As you already know, one of the things that makes the V chord so powerful is that it contains the seventh note of the scale inside it: the leading tone. That leading tone pulls up to the root of the scale and, coincidentally, the V chord pulls right to the I chord pretty much every time it's there (see **FIGURE 16-4**).

FIGURE 16-4 V Chord Leading Tone Pull

TRACK 76

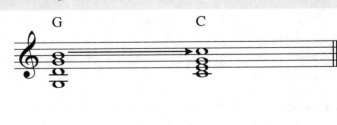

Leading Tone (B) Resolves Up To C
As V Resolves To I

This has been covered before. However, once you add the seventh to the V chord, things get more interesting. Let's go back to the key of C major as an example. The V chord is G major, and if you add a seventh to that chord it becomes G7 or V7. The notes in the chord are G B D F. What's neat, and certainly hidden unless you know to look for it, is the interval between the B and the F inside the G7 chord. The interval between B and F is a tritone, the most unstable and "grating" interval that exists. Because the G7 chord contains the tritone, it makes the chord that much more unstable, which makes the chord scream even louder, "Resolve me, please!" Let's look at how a G7 chord resolves back to C (see **FIGURE 16-5**).

FIGURE 16-5 V7 Chord Resolution

TRACK 77

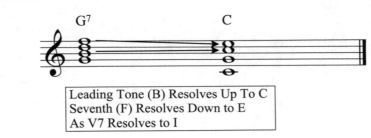

Leading Tone (B) Resolves Up To C
Seventh (F) Resolves Down to E
As V7 Resolves to I

As you can see, the leading tone of B resolves up; this is expected. The F, which is the seventh of the G7 chord, resolves down. Both the B and the F resolve in opposite directions and both resolve by half steps. While a G7 chord can be resolved other ways, and some composers certainly use other methods, this is the "expected" practice. Honestly, if you simply sit at a piano and play that chord, you'll most likely agree that letting the B go up and the F go down sounds best.

Resolving the V7 to the I chord like this highlights one of the defining principles of tonal music and chord progressions: tension and release. Music is all about tension and release. The V chord is tense to begin with; adding the seventh to it makes it even tenser, and the resolution to the I chord is the release. Composers have used this simple principle and these two chords like this for hundreds of years. Even much modern pop music contains this simple movement of V to I. Even untrained musicians can simply just "hear it."

Tonic and Dominant Melodies

For one last look at the mighty tonic and dominant chords, let's turn to the relationship of harmony to melody. You already saw how melodies and chords are closely related. Any single melody can easily be harmonized by utilizing a chord that contains a note from the melody.

Many notes of the scale can harmonize with just the I and V chords in any key. In the key of C major, the I chord takes care of the C, E, and G, while the V7 chord takes care of the notes G, B, D, and F (see **FIGURE 16-6**).

FIGURE 16-6 I and V Melodic Elements

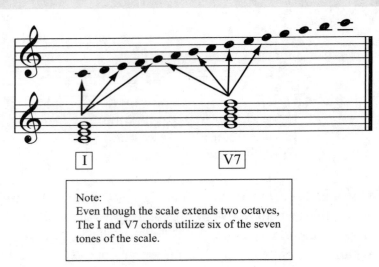

Note:
Even though the scale extends two octaves,
The I and V7 chords utilize six of the seven
tones of the scale.

Combining the notes from the I and V7 chords gives you C D E F G B. With just two chords, six out of the seven possible notes in the scale can be harmonized. The only note left hanging is the A, and that's what the other chords in the key are for.

The Other Chords

There are five more chords to know. Each chord is a unit of sound that is able to harmonize any notes that it's constructed with. In short, any triad can harmonize the three notes it's constructed with. It can, of course, do much more, but this is a good way to view chords and harmony if you've never dealt with them before. Part of the difficulty lies in the fact that any single melodic note can be harmonized so many different ways. Let's use the note G in a G major scale for example.

You can find the note G in the G major triad, the E minor triad, and the C major triad—all diatonic triads in the key of G major (see **FIGURE 16-7**). But each one produces a different sound. Let's look at a few conventions concerning how chords typically move around. Knowing how chords have been used in the last 300 or so years should give you some insight into what's been done before.

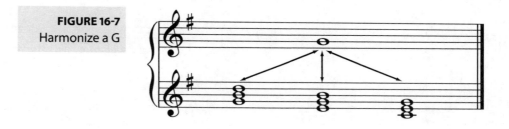

FIGURE 16-7
Harmonize a G

Movements in Fifths

One of the most accepted ways to learn about chord progressions is to use progressions that move in fifths. When you analyze a lot of music, you recognize patterns of chords moving in fifths. The first chord progression you learned about is based on the movement of a fifth. The V to I progression moves a fifth down from V to I. If you were to keep moving in fifths, you would encounter some very usable sounds.

Starting at I, moving a fifth takes us to V. A fifth from V is II. A fifth from II is VI. This progression is VI, II, V, I. Ending a chord progression with the I chord gives it some sonic closure. **FIGURE 16-8** shows what the progression sounds like in a few keys.

FIGURE 16-8 VI, II, V, I, Chord Progression

TRACK 78 | vi ii V I |

Sounds pretty nice, doesn't it? While not the only way to show chord progressions, starting from fifths is a great way to get your feet wet.

The Rest of the Chords

Let's go through all the chords in the major scale. Music theory does have fancy names for each of these chords. It's nice to know what they are if you ever enroll in a high school or college theory course.

- I Tonic—This is the chord that defines the key. You'll see it often!
- II SuperTonic—This chord typically appears before the dominant chord.
- III Mediant—A rarely used and harmonically weak chord.

- IV Subdominant—An important chord, used often.
- V Dominant—Besides tonic, the most important chord for expressing harmony.
- VI Submediant—Another chord that is used often.
- VII° Leading tone—Built on the leading tone of the scale, a chord that pulls heavily toward the tonic, much like the dominant chord does.

Primary Chords

In any key, three primary chords exist that exert the most presence and force to the scale. Those chords are I, IV, and V. Coincidentally in the major scale, all of the chords are major chords. You know that I and V is the basic chord progression and between the I and the V7 chords, six out of the seven notes of the major scale were harmonized.

But there was one lone note that wasn't harmonized. Guess what? That's what the IV chord is for! Between the I, IV, and V chords, any note on the major scale can be harmonized.

Not surprisingly, there are about 2.8 billion songs based on the mighty I, IV, V progression. Here is a partial listing of songs based around the I, IV, V progression:

- Any blues song
- "Happy Birthday"
- "Silent Night"
- "Amazing Grace"
- "La Bamba"

The I, IV, V progression is the most basic yet complete progression for providing harmony. It's no surprise that it's a staple of blues, country, folk, and classical music because of its simple, yet pleasing sounds. If you play a harmony instrument, make sure that you can play I, IV, and V chords in every key. When in doubt, those chords usually work.

The Chord Ladder

There is an interesting concept called the chord ladder that clearly explains how chords typically progress from one to another (see **FIGURE 16-9**).

This chord ladder shows the different levels of chord progressions. The I chord is the strongest chord in the key; it's the chord that shows up again and again. As you step back down the chord ladder, you can see all the possible ways to get back to I. Each level, or step on the ladder, displays another level of distance from the I chord. The farther away from I a chord is, the weaker it sounds. As you start to step back up the ladder, using a chord from each step, you are able to craft some nice chord progressions.

The chord ladder is also useful for showing options. Certain steps on the ladder contain two different chords, such as I and VI. This means that these two chords can be used in place of each other—as long as the melody supports it. You are getting your first taste of chord substitution: being able to harmonize the same melody note with another chord.

These are not the only ways to write chord progressions. We haven't even talked about the minor key yet, which is covered in the next chapter.

FIGURE 16-9 Chord Ladder

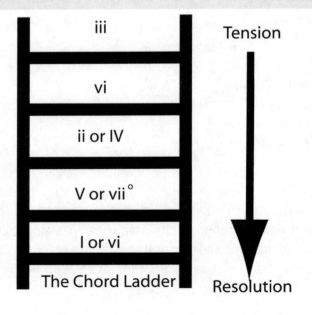

Chapter 17

E

Advanced Chord Progressions

Y ou've come a long way in music theory by now. The next stage in your journey is the study of more advanced harmonic progressions. Minor key progressions, chord substitutions, cadences, chord inversions, and basic reharmonization are the next steps toward harmonic freedom.

Minor Keys

By now you've got a good understanding of the dominant chords (I and V). It's time to take the leap to the minor key. Are minor keys that different from major? The one principal difference of minor keys is that the V chord must be altered and made major in order for the chord progressions to sound "traditional." Traditional music theory always uses a major V chord, whether you're in a major key or a minor key.

Simply making every V chord major and harmonizing in the minor key is enough. The chord ladder remains the same—the only thing that changes is the quality of the chords. **FIGURE 17-1** shows the chord ladder for the minor key.

FIGURE 17-1 Minor Key Chord Ladder

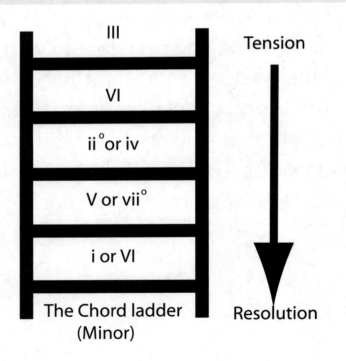

Melodic Minor Harmony

Remember the melodic minor scale? See **FIGURE 17-2**.

FIGURE 17-2 Melodic Minor Scale

What was the defining characteristic about melodic minor? If you remember from Chapter 12, the melodic minor scale started out as a traditional natural minor scale and was altered by raising the sixth and seventh notes up a half step. Every time a note in the scale is changed, all of the harmony created with that scale is also affected. Just as harmonic minor affected the V chord by making it major, melodic minor has the interesting effect of making the IV and the V chords major, which yields a different sound for the minor key. **FIGURE 17-3** is an example in D minor using the IV and V chords.

FIGURE 17-3 D Minor Progression I, IV, V, I

TRACK 79

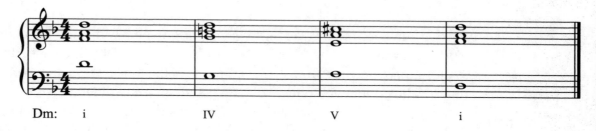

It's a nice progression that sounds like a fusion between major and minor. It includes the bright IV and V chords, with the darker resolution of the minor I chord. This is used often, especially in classical music.

Substitute Chords

A substitute chord, or a substitution, is when you choose to replace a preexisting chord or reharmonize a melody with a different chord. The chord ladder is the best place to look for this. **FIGURE 17-4** shows the major chord ladder again.

FIGURE 17-4 Major Chord Ladder

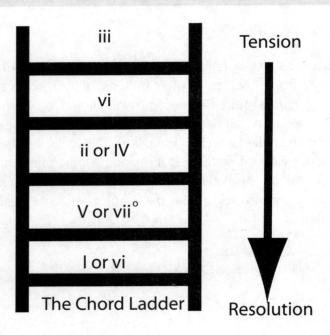

On any step of the ladder, a chord is grouped with another chord specifically because they share notes, usually two out of the three notes that make a triad. Because they share two-thirds of the tones, they can typically be substituted for each other. You can get an amazing difference in sound when you utilize chord substitution. **FIGURE 17-5** is a simple melody that you will recognize, arranged two different ways. The first is using traditional chords—this is the way it's usually heard. The subsequent passage reharmonizes the melody with substitute chords. What do you think of the changes? Whether or not you agree with all of them, the chords serve their functions as suitable harmony in both cases.

FIGURE 17-5 Reharmonization

TRACK 80

Original Harmony

Reharmonization

Look at the piece and see why those chords were chosen. Do a little bit of analysis on your own to figure this out. You have all the tools; just spend some time looking at this music. In general, when you hear something interesting, something that you find intriguing, try to break it apart to figure out what is going on in the music. This is generally the way of theory: Music comes first, and theory comes after we look back and try to figure out what's going on.

Cadences

A cadence is the end of a musical phrase or the end of a musical section. A cadence is a grouping of a few chords that end an idea or section. Cadences are found at spots where the music wants to rest or come to some sort of conclusion. In traditional tonal music, there are only a few types of cadences and, not surprisingly, most revolve around the idea of the dominant resolving to the tonic.

Authentic Cadence

An authentic cadence is a specific kind of closing cadence that progresses from V to I. What makes a traditional authentic cadence so strong is that the top note in both chords is preset. In the V chord the third must be in the highest voice, and in the I chord the root must be in the highest voice (see **FIGURE 17-6**).

FIGURE 17-6 Authentic Cadence

TRACK 81

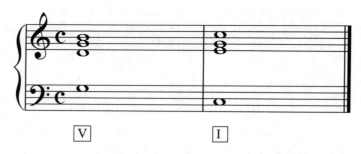

The movement from B to C, a half step, in the highest voice is what makes this progression "authentic," especially in terms of traditional music theory. However, for most people, just the progression of V to I is enough to sound "authentic" regardless of the individual voice leading. Just know that if you study theory in a class, there are specific rules you need to be aware of. In other styles of music, or your own personal music, you are free to make your own decisions.

Plagal Cadence

The plagal cadence is a specific kind of resolution cadence. In a plagal cadence, the IV chord resolves to the I chord. The term plagal is used to describe a place of worship. The plagal cadence is most popular for its use at the end of many church hymns. The familiar "Amen" that is sung at the end of almost every hymn in church music is always based on the plagal cadence of IV to I. It is written out in **FIGURE 17-7**.

FIGURE 17-7 Plagal Cadence

TRACK 82

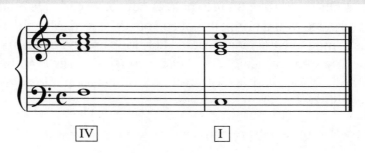

IV   I

Plagal cadences originated in the church, but their use is not limited to such. Many pop and rock songs utilize IV to I cadences at the end of phrases and songs. If you ever find yourself at a church, listen for the plagal cadence—it's all over the place!

Deceptive Cadence

A deceptive cadence is a "fake out." You begin with the ubiquitous V chord, which should resolve to I. Instead, in a deceptive cadence, the V is resolved to VI (see **FIGURE 17-8**), which is a substitute for the I chord. This progression plays upon the fact that the V chord is an unstable chord that needs to be resolved. Since it is resolved in a "deceptive" way, it plays upon the weakness of the VI chord. Musicians sometimes use this when they are writing a phrase that's not quite ready to end yet and they need to "keep it alive" a little longer. A VI chord is a lovely substitute for a I chord.

TRACK 83

FIGURE 17-8 Deceptive Cadence

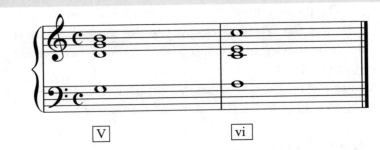

V   vi

One important thing to note: A deceptive cadence is not a final cadence, as a piece would normally not end on a VI chord. After the deceptive cadence is completed, the piece would likely loop around again and eventually close with an ear pleasing V to I cadence (see **FIGURE 17-9**). In this case, the VI chord is followed up with a II, V, I progression, closing with an authentic cadence.

FIGURE 17-9 Deceptive Cadence with Final Resolution

TRACK 84

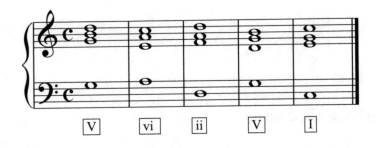

V   vi   ii   V   I

Half Cadence

As you can probably guess from its title, the half cadence is not an ending cadence; rather, it's a cadence used at the end of a phrase that continues on. A half cadence is any cadence that ends on V (see **FIGURE 17-10**). Typically, a half cadence is either II, V or IV, V. Because the cadence ends on the V chord, which is fairly unstable and needs to continue forward, it's only "half" done. At some other point down the road, the music will be completed and will close with a final cadence. Since cadences are loosely defined as a points of rest, musicians use half cadences at points that take brief pauses and continue forward.

FIGURE 17-10 Half Cadence

TRACK 85

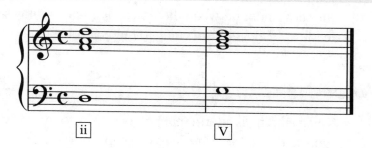

Inversions

A chord inversion is simply any time a note other than the root is in the lowest voice of the chord. Typically, the third or the fifth are in the lowest voice (first and second inversion). Many students find it hard to understand why a composer would ever want to invert a chord. For many players, especially piano and guitar players who play alone, chords are almost always in root position, as they sound "fullest" that way. But there must be reasons why they are used. Of course there are! In a word: smooth.

Why Use Chord Inversions?

Chord inversions exist to smooth out harmony. Triads in root position may tend to jump around in the music, which can sometimes sound discordant and awkward. The simplest way to understand chord inversions is to think about the smoothness. Let's take an example of a simple I, IV, V, I progression in the key of A major (see **FIGURE 17-11**).

FIGURE 17-11 Root Position Triads

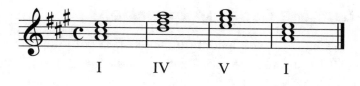

If all the chords are kept in root position, the bass notes and the triads themselves tend to skip around a lot. If a composer wants to smooth out the movement between the notes, he must employ something called voice leading. Inversions are going to help us voice lead!

Voice Leading

Voice leading is a term that harkens back to the early days of writing music: writing music for choir. When composers wrote for choir, the trend was to make the voices move smoothly from note to note. Frequent skips were difficult for many untrained choirs to handle. The smoother the musical lines, the better it sounded.

Let's use our previous example, **FIGURE 17-11**, and see how voice leading can enhance it. Instead of just stringing together triads, let's try to move to the closest available note in the next chord. Take a look at the example with arrows to show you how the notes smoothly lead from one to another (see **FIGURE 17-12**).

FIGURE 17-12 Voice Lead Triads

TRACK 86

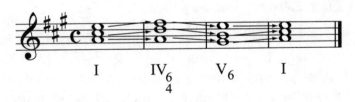

$$\text{I} \qquad \text{IV}_6^4 \qquad \text{V}_6 \qquad \text{I}$$

As you can see, and more importantly hear, this example sounds polished. You can see that few of the chords are left in their original forms. These are a whole bunch of chord inversions. Let's look at this more closely.

Voice Leading Leads to Inversions

Using the voice leading in **FIGURE 17-12** came up with a much different piece. Gone were the root position triads that jumped around from chord to chord; now the piece has a smooth sound. The progression is still I, IV, V, I. That hasn't changed. However, the inversions are as follows.

- Chord #1 = A major chord, root position.
- Chord #2 = D major chord, second inversion: By putting the IV chord in its second inversion, we kept the A in the bass for the first and the second chords.
- Chord #3 = E major chord, first inversion: Using a first inversion V chord led the bass from the preceding note of A down a half step to G♯. This kept the bass movement very small and smooth.
- Chord #4 = A major chord, root position.

A phrase or cadence typically will end with a I chord in root position. The overall bass movement of this example has been A, A, G♯, A—smooth indeed! Not only is the bass movement smoother, but all the voices are smoother now.

Smooth Bass

Voice leading is very useful in writing music, especially classical and jazz music. However, it's not always applicable to every style of music. In rock music, true voice leading is rare and it makes chord inversions equally rare for that very reason. One of the other uses of inversions is to smooth out the bass lines of a chord progression. If you play guitar, this sort of voice leading and inversion may be the best you can muster on the instrument— the guitar is very hard to properly voice lead due to the limitation of how the instrument is tuned and played. In any case, you can do some cool things with inversions and bass lines. Let's crack this from two angles. The first is by building a chord progression starting with just a bass line. The second will be to enhance a pre-existing chord progression.

Starting with a Bass Line

We're going to start with a bass line and then construct a chord progression around it using some inverted chords. For simplicity's sake, our bass line will go right up a G major scale. **FIGURE 17-13** shows the bass line as it stands right now.

FIGURE 17-13 Simple Bass Line

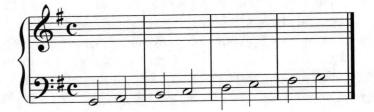

It would be a crashing bore to use all of those notes in the bass for root position triads. Music rarely moves by step up the scale like that. What we can do is use chord inversions to harmonize this line. See **FIGURE 17-14** for just one way to do this.

FIGURE 17-14 Bass Line Harmonized

TRACK 87

I V₆₄ I₆ IV V IV₆ V₆ I

As you can see from the analysis below the chords, we used a combination of I, IV, and V chords in this progression, utilizing a few different inversions of each. The result is pretty neat. Doing this gives us a musically interesting bass line while still keeping the harmony fairly simple and palatable using only primary chords.

The other way to do this is to smooth out a pre-existing chord progression. **FIGURE 17-15** shows another simple I, IV, V, I progression.

FIGURE 17-15 Simple Chord Progression

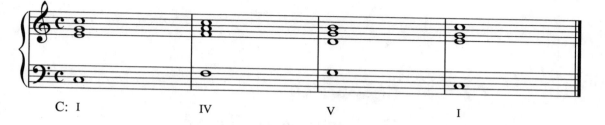

In this case, we're going to use chord inversions to move the bass lines up in a smoother fashion and create a sense of movement. To do this, we will now extend the length of all of the chords. In addition, when the bass line moves, we can change the configuration of those chords to better fit the new voice leading. Even though the example looks a little different than what we started with, all we did is lengthen the chords that were already there by adding inversions to create a sense of movement (see **FIGURE 17-16**). What's cool is that the progression sounds as if it's moving around, when the chords don't actually move, only their bass notes and corresponding inversions do. This is a useful technique.

FIGURE 17-16 Simple Chord Progression with Inversions

TRACK 88

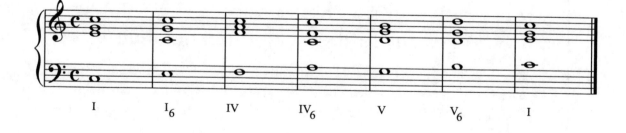

Chapter 18
Other Scales

So much of music theory relies on the tried and true major and minor scales. In the grand breadth of music, other scales exist and are commonly used. Whether you compose, improvise jazz, or just want to understand all the possibilities of melodic composition, knowledge of additional scales will further your mind and ear.

Modes

The first place to deepen your understanding of scales is right back at the major scale. Modes is a term you may or may not have heard as a musician. Many classical musicians don't deal with modes early on in their study. However, jazz and rock players are aware of modes early on. There are several reasons for this musical divide, which will become clear as you learn more about modes.

The simplest way to define a mode is as a displaced major scale. Let's examine what displaced means. Take the C major scale (C D E F G A B C). Many examples in this book show melodies and harmonies composed using this scale. What makes it a C scale is that the note C has the most weight; the piece keeps coming back to C. Now, what if you were to use the same vocabulary—i.e., use the same C D E F G A B C pitches—but instead make a different note the root? What if the scale looked like this: D E F G A B C D? If the scale looked like that and D sounded like the root note, then you'd have an official "mode." A mode is formed when you call any other note besides the original root of the scale the root. Because a major scale has seven notes, there are seven modes.

Modes gained prominence during the golden age of Gregorian chant, circa A.D. 900, when they were used to compose the melodies of vocal plainchant. Modes stayed in use throughout Medieval times with some modification. The Baroque and pre-Baroque eras made use of major and minor scales instead of modes. For all intents and purposes, modes lay dormant throughout Baroque, Classical, and most of the Romantic era. Even though impressionist composers revived modes, it wasn't until jazz musicians started using modes in improvisation and composition that modes became a useful part of music curricula. Nowadays, all music students learn about modes, but it's the rock and jazz players who tend to utilize them more frequently in improvisation and composition than anyone else.

Seven Modal Scales

Each and every major scale can be looked at from seven different angles— one mode starting from each note in the scale. While modes theoretically come from "parent" major scales, it's easiest to think of them as their own entities.

Ionian

Ionian is the first mode to learn about—and, thankfully, you already know it. The Ionian scale is simply the major scale. It follows the interval pattern **WWHWWWH**. **FIGURE 18-1** shows a G Ionian mode. Since the Ionian mode is simply the traditional major scale, this example is just a definition of the word Ionian.

FIGURE 18-1 Ionian Mode

Dorian

The Dorian mode is the first of the displaced scales. The easiest way to define Dorian is that a Dorian scale is a major scale played from its second note. If you continue to use G major as the "parent" scale, the Dorian mode in this key starts from the note A and progress up the same notes. **FIGURE 18-2** shows the A Dorian scale. The A Dorian scale uses the interval pattern **WHWWWHW**.

FIGURE 18-2 Dorian Mode

TRACK 89

There is a very important aspect to understand about modes. Yes, it is true that the A Dorian scale comes from the G major scale and shares all the same notes. This is an important learning tool. Musicians need to learn the modes as things separate from the major scales. The A Dorian mode is a scale unto itself with its own distinct sound. If you look at the notes of A Dorian (A B C D E F♯ G A), you might notice that the A Dorian scale looks a lot like the traditional A minor scale. And you're right, it looks just like it! The only difference is that the A Dorian scale contains an F♯ and the A minor scale contains an F♮.

You could look at the A Dorian scale as a minor type scale, with an altered sixth note. In this case, the sixth note is raised up a half step. It's very much like a "flavored" minor scale. This is how modes are used today—to spice up traditional major and minor scales that may sound overused and dated. As you'll see, all of the rest of the modes will closely resemble either a traditional major or a traditional minor scale.

Phrygian

Phrygian is the third mode and is the result of forming a scale starting from the third note of the parent major scale. Using G major as the parent scale, the Phrygian scale is a B Phrygian scale. It uses the interval pattern **HWWWHWW**. (See **FIGURE 18-3**.) Phrygian has a distinct sound and sometimes recalls the music of Spain, as Spanish composers often use this scale.

FIGURE 18-3 Phrygian Mode

The B Phrygian scale (B C D E F♯ G A B) looks very much like a traditional B minor scale (B C♯ D E F♯ G A B). The only difference is that a B Phrygian scale lowers the second note a half step down. You could say that Phrygian is just a minor scale with a lowered second note—and you'd be right!

Lydian

The fourth mode of the major scale is the Lydian mode. Using G as a parent scale, we come to the C Lydian scale. Lydian uses the interval pattern **WWWHWWH**. (See **FIGURE 18-4**.)

FIGURE 18-4 Lydian Mode

The Lydian mode is a striking, beautiful, and "bright" sound. It's used by film composers to convey uplifting spirit and is a favorite of jazz and rock composers. The Lydian scale is so bright and happy, it's no surprise that it's closely related to the major scale. The C Lydian scale is spelled C D E F♯ G A B C, which resembles a traditional C major scale (C D E F G A B C). The only difference between C Lydian and C major is that a Lydian scale raises the fourth note of the major scale up a half step. C Lydian is a C major scale with a raised fourth note. The raised fourth tone has a bright and unusual sound and allows the plain major scale to have a unique overall effect.

Mixolydian

The fifth mode of the major scale is called the Mixolydian mode. Using the parent scale of G, our fifth mode is D Mixolydian. D Mixolydian, or mixo as it's commonly abbreviated, uses the interval pattern of **WWHWWHW**. (See **FIGURE 18-5**.) The Mixolydian mode is a mainstay of jazz, rock, and blues music.

FIGURE 18-5 Mixolydian Mode

TRACK 92

The Mixolydian mode is closely related to the major scale, but is slightly darker sounding. The D Mixolydian scale (D E F♯ G A B C D) closely resembles the D major scale (D E F♯ G A B C♯ D). The only difference is that the Mixolydian scale lowers the seventh note of the major scale a half step. The lowered seventh note gives the Mixolydian mode a bluesy, dark color—leading away from the overly peppy major scale. Because of this, it's a staple of blues, rock, and jazz players looking to darken up the sound of major scales. It also coincides with one of the principal chords of jazz, blues, and rock music: the dominant seventh chord (D7).

Aeolian

The sixth mode of the major scale is the Aeolian mode. If you remember back to the section on minor scales earlier in this book, you'll remember that minor scales are derived from the sixth note of a major scale. That's right, the Aeolian mode is the natural minor scale. Thankfully, this is another mode that you already know. Aeolian is the proper name for natural minor. Using the parent key of G major, our sixth mode brings us to E Aeolian. You'll also remember that the keys of G major and E minor are "related keys"—G Ionian and E Aeolian are related modes from the same parent scale. The E Aeolian scale uses the interval formula **WHWWHWW**. (See **FIGURE 18-6**.)

FIGURE 18-6 Aeolian Mode

Since the Aeolian scale is an exact minor scale, no comparison to another major or minor scale is needed. Even with that, some players are more comfortable with major scales; Aeolian can be looked at as a major scale with a lowered third, sixth, and seventh note. This way of looking at minor scales is useful to some.

Locrian

The seventh and final mode is called the Locrian mode. In our parent scale of G major, the seventh mode is F♯ Locrian. The F♯ Locrian mode uses the interval pattern **HWWHWWW**. (See **FIGURE 18-7**.) The Locrian mode has a very distinct sound. You're not going to encounter this mode often. Actually, you may go your whole life without ever hearing it or using it. Nevertheless, it completes your knowledge of modes, so it's useful.

FIGURE 18-7 Locrian Mode

TRACK 93

The F♯ Locrian scale (F♯ G A B C D E F♯) looks a lot like an F♯ minor scale (F♯ G♯ A B C♯ D E F♯). The only difference between the two scales is that the Locrian scale has a lowered second and lowered fifth note.

Looking at Modes on Their Own

The modes that you know, you know in relation to a parent scale. If someone were to ask you to spell a C   Lydian scale, you might have to go through quite an ordeal. First, you have to remember which number mode it is, then you have to backtrack and find the parent scale, and then you can spell the scale correctly. It's much more convenient to think of the modes on their own, which is how they are usually used. It's much easier to make one step to understand modes than to always have to take five steps. Looking at modes as an "almost" major or minor scale will help you understand modes.

Here is a recap of the modes, their interval formulas, and easy ways to relate the scales:

- Mode 1—Ionian (**WWHWWWH**). Ionian is the major scale.
- Mode 2—Dorian (**WHWWWHW**). Dorian is a minor scale with a raised sixth tone.
- Mode 3—Phrygian (**HWWWHWW**). Phrygian is a minor scale with a lowered second tone.

- Mode 4—Lydian (**WWWHWWH**). Lydian is a major scale with a raised fourth note.
- Mode 5—Mixolydian (**WWHWWHW**). Mixolydian is a major scale with a lowered seventh tone.
- Mode 6—Aeolian (**WHWWHWW**). Aeolian is the minor scale.
- Mode 7—Locrian (**HWWHWWW**). Locrian is a minor scale with a lowered second and fifth tone.

By learning these formulas, you will be able to learn modes as their own scales and spell and relate them quickly and easily.

Other Important Scales

Major scales and modes make up the majority of the scales encountered in Western music. However, they are not the only important scales. There are more scales than you could imagine!

Major Pentatonic

Pentatonic scales differ from traditional major and minor scales in that they contain only five notes per octave as opposed to major and minor scales that contain seven. The name Pentatonic reflects this distinction, as the prefix of Pentatonic is Penta, Greek for five, and tonic means tones or notes. The pentatonic scales are widely used in folk, liturgical, rock, and jazz music. Pentatonic scales come into two varieties: major and minor.

The major pentatonic is a five-note scale that is related to the major scale. It simply omits two notes—the fourth and seventh tones—from the major scale. In the key of C, the major pentatonic scale is C D E G A C. Another way is to say that C major pentatonic is the first, second, third, fifth, and sixth notes of a major scale. (See **FIGURE 18-8**.)

FIGURE 18-8 Major Pentatonic Scale

Major Pentatonic

The major pentatonic is a mainstay of folk, blues, rock, and country music. Famous melodies such as "Amazing Grace" were composed solely using the major pentatonic scale. If you improvise solos, such as rock, jazz, or blues solos, the major pentatonic is a basic and essential scale for improvisation over major tonalities.

Minor Pentatonic

The minor pentatonic is another five-tone scale. Like its relative the major pentatonic scale, the minor pentatonic scale is a minor scale with two notes omitted. To form a minor pentatonic scale, simply leave out the second and sixth tones from a natural (Aeolian!) minor scale. In the key of C, a minor pentatonic scale is (C E♭ F G B♭ C). You could also say that the scale is the first, third, fourth, fifth, and seventh notes of a minor scale. (See **FIGURE 18-9**.)

FIGURE 18-9 Minor Pentatonic Scale

Minor Pentatonic

If you learn to improvise in any style, this is the scale you need to learn. It is the mainstay of every style of music imaginable and is the primary scale found in most, if not all, rock and blues improvisations. A very important scale to know!

The Blues Scale

The blues scale is a very simple variation of the minor pentatonic. The blues scale adds an additional note to the minor pentatonic scale. In the blues scale, a chromatic tone is inserted between the fourth and fifth tones. In the key of C, the blues scale is C E♭ F G♭ G♮ B♭. (See **FIGURE 18-10**.) Adding this one tone to the minor pentatonic instantly yields a more bluesy sound.

FIGURE 18-10 Minor Blues Scale

TRACK 96

Blues Scale

Whole Tone

The whole tone scale is a particular type of scale called a symmetric scale. The whole tone scale is built entirely with whole steps. Because it uses the same intervals, the whole tone scale is considered symmetric. Using whole steps from C, a C whole tone scale is C D E F♯ G♯ A♯. (See **FIGURE 18-11**.) This is a six-note scale.

FIGURE 18-11 Whole Tone Scale

TRACK 97

Whole Tone Scale

Of particular interest is that there are only two different whole tone scales. Forming whole tone scales from anywhere other than C or C♯ will yield the exact same notes as the C or C♯ whole tone scales. Try it yourself! Whole tones scales are unusual-sounding scales. They are frequently used in cartoon and film music during dream sequences due to their dreamy, unique sound. Romantic era composers and jazz players dig 'em too!

Chromatic

The chromatic scale is an easy scale. It uses every chromatic pitch (twelve in all) in order. (See **FIGURE 18-12**.)

FIGURE 18-12 Chromatic Scale

TRACK 98

Chromatic Scale

Diminished/Octatonic Scales

The last scale is another symmetric scale and is built using repeating intervals. The diminished scale is based on repeating intervals, always half steps and whole steps. There are two varieties of diminished scales: one that starts with the pattern whole step, half step intervals and one that uses half step, whole step interval patterns. **FIGURE 18-13** shows the two varieties of diminished scales, both starting from C. The other name that diminished scales go by is octatonic, which is Greek for "eight-note scale." This is the first scale that exceeds seven individual notes.

FIGURE 18-13 Diminished Scales

TRACK 99

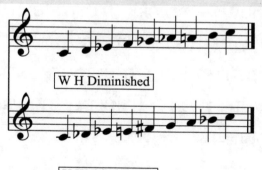

W H Diminished

H W Diminished

Another interesting fact is that there are only three unique diminished scales. Diminished scales spelled from C, C♯, and D are the only diminished scales that utilize unique tone sets. Spelling diminished scales from other roots will yield repeating scales, with the identical tones from C, C♯, or D diminished. Composers, theorists, and jazz players use diminished scales primarily.

Chapter 19

Transposing Instruments

One of the most confusing and maligned aspects of music theory is the nature of transposing instruments. Few topics frustrate students more than this. There is a long history of why instruments transpose and how to deal with them. Transposing isn't difficult, only misunderstood.

What Is Transposing?

Suppose John plays the alto saxophone and Tara plays the trumpet. They get together and jam one day. John writes a short melody on the sax, notates it, and hands it to Tara to play along. To their shock and amazement, the resulting sound is terrible. What was supposed to be two instruments playing the same melody in concert ended up as a cacophony! Confused, they set out to understand why alto sax and trumpet can't read the same melody. What they discover is that transposing and the natural keys of instruments have caused this musical calamity. All their lives, John and Tara were taught that C is C and D is D and so on. Unfortunately, this is not true.

Concert Pitch

The pitch of any note is a mathematical event. Notes exist as vibrations of air. The speed at which they vibrate can be measured and is expressed in Hertz (Hz). This is the only true measure of a note—its frequency in Hz. A large group of instruments exist that play in "concert pitch," meaning that when they play or read a note on the musical staff, they are getting the "mathematically correct" answer. When a piano plays a middle C, it's playing a note with a frequency of 261 Hz—it's an exact thing; the piano is playing "concert pitch." There are a large number of instruments that play concert pitch. Here is a list of popular instruments that play concert pitch. These are also called C instruments:

- Violin, viola, cello, bass*
- Piano
- Harp
- Guitar*
- Flute
- Oboe
- Bassoon
- Trombone
- Baritone horn
- Tuba
- Pitched percussion

The entire preceding list plays in concert key. There are two exceptions: Guitar and bass transpose an octave in order to keep their music in the staff, but they are still considered concert—more on this later.

FACT

A great example of a concert pitch is an orchestral tuning note. When a symphony orchestra tunes up, the oboe player plays a concert A note. The rest of the orchestra tunes up to this concert A note. Most metronomes that provide a tuning pitch also provide the same concert A (A = 440 Hz).

Here is a list of the common instruments that transpose:

- Clarinet
- Soprano, alto, tenor, and baritone saxophone
- French horn
- Trumpet

This is it for the "common" instruments. There are more transposing instruments, and a good orchestration book would set you up with all the answers.

What Does Transposing Mean?

A transposing instrument reads the exact same music as other instruments. The only difference is that when a trumpet plays a written C, the note that comes out of the trumpet would not register as a C on a tuner or match a C on a piano. An entirely different note comes out! A concert B♭ is heard when a trumpet plays a written C. This is what is meant by "transposition." Let's look at an example. If you play a short melody for the trumpet on the top staff, what you actually hear is the bottom staff! (See **FIGURE 19-1**.)

FIGURE 19-1
Transposing
Melody

Trumpet Reads:

We Hear These Notes:

Now you start to see the possibility for confusion. If you didn't know about this, you might be very perplexed. Just think about poor Tara and John. Amazingly, this isn't always taught in the study of an instrument. Most students just learn to read the notes in front of them.

Why Does This Happen?

Good question. Why can't we all just get along—er, play in the same key? The reasons that certain instruments transpose and others don't are covered by one of two answers. The first answer is history. Brass instruments rely heavily on the overtone series to make their notes happen. Brass instruments used to add crooks, which were additional pipes, to their instruments in order to play in different keys. The French horn was a good example of this. In time, as the instruments evolved and valves were added to the brass instruments, the additional crooks were no longer necessary. Certain instruments evolved into certain keys and stayed there. It's now been so long and there has been so much music written that it would be very painful to change.

The second reason is best shown in the sax family. There are four saxophones in common use today: soprano, alto, tenor, and baritone. Each of the four saxophones transposes differently. The reason that it's done this way has less to do with history and more with ease of the player. Each of the four saxophones, while physically differing in size, have the exact same system of keys that Adolph Sax invented in the 1800s. The sax transposes four different ways so that any sax player trained on any one of the instruments could play any of the saxophones without having to relearn anything. Each saxophone reads the same treble clef melody and the composer makes sure that each part is transposed correctly on paper for the proper sonic result. Some other instruments also do this.

ESSENTIAL

Think you're immune from this? Play in a rock band? Imagine this: You play in a blues band and you bring in a sax or trumpet player to expand your sound. When it comes time to teach them the melodies, what are you going to tell them to play? They want to solo on the E blues your guitar player is so fond of? Exactly what will you say to them? You need to know how transposition works.

Transposing Chant

For too many years, students have been baffled, perplexed, and generally confused as to how to transpose correctly for instruments. But you can learn a chant that will help you make sense of it. The answer lies in knowing two things: You have to know the full name of the instrument and you have to know the chant.

Each instrument has a key name. But a trumpet isn't usually called a B♭ trumpet, is it? "Trumpet" usually suffices. Knowing the full name of each of the instruments is the key to understanding how they transpose. The other is the chant, which goes like this:

The instrument key name is the note that you hear in concert pitch when that instrument reads its written C.

Let's put that to use, using the B♭ trumpet again, which has a key name of B♭. To understand how the chant helps, add this information into your chant: The instrument key name (in this case B♭) is the note you hear in concert pitch when that instrument (trumpet) reads its written C. Simply, when a trumpet plays a written C, you hear a B♭. (See **FIGURE 19-2**.)

FIGURE 19-2 Trumpet Transpose

Trumpet Reads:

We Hear:

This means that whatever note or notes are written for trumpet will come out exactly one whole step below what is written. So what can composers do to fix this? Simply write the trumpet part up a whole step, in a written D. The trumpet player will read and play the D, yet a perfect C will come out in concert key.

Sound down, write up. For most instruments this is the case. There are a couple of zany exceptions, but you don't need to worry about them right now. For the most part, you write parts up and they sound down. Just remember the chant.

B♭ Instruments

There are a few common instruments that exist in the key of B♭ together and thus transpose the exact same way. The B♭ instruments include the

FIGURE 19-3 B♭ Transpose

B♭ Instruments Read:

We Hear:

B♭ trumpet, B♭ clarinet, and B♭ soprano saxophone. Each of these instruments follows the same rule: Whatever they read comes out a whole step down. (See **FIGURE 19-3**.)

There is another instrument that is called a B♭ instrument: the B♭ tenor sax. It's a little bit different than the others—it transposes an octave and a whole step down. When a tenor sax plays a C, you indeed hear a B♭, but it's a full octave lower than the other

FIGURE 19-4 Tenor Sax Transpose

B♭ Instruments Read:

We Hear:

B♭ instruments. (See **FIGURE 19-4**.) To write parts that sound correct, you have to write the part up a whole step in the case of clarinet, trumpet, and soprano sax. In the case of tenor sax, write it up an octave and a whole step (or a major ninth).

E♭ Instruments

There are two common instruments that are in the key of E♭: the E♭ alto saxophone and the E♭ baritone saxophone. Being in the key of E♭ means

FIGURE 19-5 Alto Sax Transpose

Alto Sax Reads:

We Hear:

that when these instruments read a written C, an E♭. concert pitch is heard. The E♭ alto saxophone transposes a major sixth away from where it's written. (See **FIGURE 19-5**.) This means that a melody written in concert pitch would have to be transposed up a major sixth in order to sound correct on the alto saxophone.

FIGURE 19-6 Baritone Sax Transpose

The baritone saxophone is also in the key of E♭; the only difference is that the baritone is a full octave below the alto sax, so it transposes at the intervals of a major sixth and an octave (or a major thirteenth). (See **FIGURE 19-6**.) In order for a melody written in concert key to sound correctly on a baritone sax, it must be written a major thirteenth up! Remember, it sounds down, but it must be written up.

F Instruments

Two instruments transpose in the key of F: the French horn and the English horn. Both the French horn and the English horn transpose in the same

FIGURE 19-7 French/English Horn Transpose

way, exactly a fifth away. (See **FIGURE 19-7**.) If a composer writes a melody in concert key and wants the French horn and English horn to play it correctly, he must write the melody up a perfect fifth in order for it to sound correct.

Octave Transposes

The guitar and bass are unique transposing instruments. Both the guitar and the bass play in concert key. That is, when guitar and bass play the note C, an electronic tuner would register the note C. But the guitar and bass "octave transpose"—that is, the pitch they read is an octave higher than the sound that comes out of the instruments. (See **FIGURE 19-8**.) This is a slightly unusual practice. The reason for this makes perfect sense! If guitar and bass did not transpose like this, their music would be extremely low on the staff—most of the notes they played would be many ledger lines below the staff. And you know how annoying it is to read that way. Guitar and bass raise their notes an octave higher to keep the majority of the notes on the staff for ease of reading.

You could go your whole life never knowing this and you may never even notice! If you ever have to write a unison line for guitar or bass, you'll know exactly what to do.

FIGURE 19-8 Guitar and Bass Transpose

Guitar/Bass Reads:

We Hear:

Note:
Bass reads in bass clef, both transpose the same interval.

Practice

Transposing is a skill that can be a tad confusing! **FIGURES 19-9**, **19-10**, and **19-11** give a few examples to help you practice. Feel free to write in the book with pencil! The first note in each example is provided for you. You'll find the answers to these examples in Appendix C at the end of the book.

Hint: The trumpet is in the key of B♭. You'll have to rewrite the melody in the correct key. Remember, sound down, write up!

FIGURE 19-9 Trumpet Transposing Practice

Hint: The French horn is in the key of F. You'll have to rewrite the melody in the correct key. Remember, sound down, write up!

FIGURE 19-10 French Horn Transposing Practice

Hint: The alto sax is in the key of E♭. You'll have to rewrite the melody in the correct key. Remember, sound down, write up!

FIGURE 19-11 Alto Sax Transposing Practice

Chapter 20

Musical Shorthand: Reading Lead Sheets

In addition to the standard written music that you have studied thus far, another style of writing music is in use today—the lead sheet. While it borrows its symbology from standard written music, a lead sheet has its own system to learn and decipher. If you ever plan to play jazz, popular, or pit band music, you need to know about lead sheets. In many cases, you may read lead sheets more often than standard notation.

Standard Notation

Standard notation has been around for a long, long time. There is no need to change it. It has evolved into a clear system for representing music. Even with the implied perfection of the standard system, other forms of written music exist. Lead sheets can apply to any instrument, and they are common musical shorthand nowadays.

FIGURE 20-1 Lead Sheet Example

FIGURE 20-1 shows a standard lead sheet. There are a few subvarieties that will be covered later, but this is the most common. What do you see in **FIGURE 20-1**? For starters, there is a standard single-line melody, in this case "Jingle Bells." Above the standard melody line are basic chord symbols. These symbols correspond to the chords you have learned in this book and are able to spell and play. That is the only surface information displayed in a standard lead sheet. However, you can make more music than you think using this information. A drummer can create a drum part from this

and a bass player can easily construct a bass line from the chord symbols. A lead sheet provides a skeleton of sorts. One basic melody line with chord symbols can be enough musical fuel for several players to play full-blown arrangements. The large majority of jazz music is notated this way. Remember that the next time you hear a jazz group—it's pretty amazing.

From one lead sheet (melody with chord symbols), a musician can construct the following parts:

- Melody (sung or played)
- Chord accompaniment (piano/guitar)
- Bass line
- Drum accompaniment

The Elements

How do you go from a basic lead sheet to full-blown musical perfection? A lead sheet can be a simple melody (à la "Jingle Bells"), or in the case of jazz music, can prove rather difficult.

The Melody

The melody is the most clear-cut part of a lead sheet. What you see is generally what you get. A lead sheet is typically a single-note melody line. Most, if not all, lead sheets are assumed to be in concert key (the key of C). If you play one of the transposing instruments you learned about in Chapter 19, then you may have to transpose the melody accordingly if you want to play it. Often, you find lead sheets in large collections of popular and folk tunes. If this is the case, you may also find versions in B♭ and E♭ so that transposing isn't necessary. The melodic element is the clearest displayed element of a lead sheet. Not much more to know—play the melody line as written.

Chord Symbols

Above the melody are shorthand chord symbols. You are used to seeing chords written out as stacks of vertical notes. But instead of being in standard notation, chords can be displayed as symbols of text (e.g., G, Cm, A7). The reason this works is because the typical chordal instruments (guitar/piano) are typically more comfortable playing chords by symbols, rather than reading them. This is especially true for guitar. When a composer provides a chord symbol, she leaves it up to the player to realize his or her own voicing of the particular chord. As you remember, there are many, many ways to play any chord. Using chord symbols not only removes the need for the player to read vertical stacks of notes, it also visually streamlines and simplifies the lead sheet.

Chord Categories

On a lead sheet, the chords are written in shorthand. There are several common symbols that you should know. These examples will all use the key of C for simplicity, but the information applies to any key.

- Major Chords. Major chords are typically displayed as a single uppercase letter. You also may see C major written out as C major or CM (the uppercase M is important) or Cmaj. In some jazz charts, major is also signified with a small triangle: C△ = C major. Typically it's just a single uppercase letter.
- Minor Chords. Minor chords have less variation in their writing style. It's either Cm or C- for C minor. Both the lowercase m and the - signify minor chords.
- Diminished Chords. Diminished chords appear typically as C° or C dim. You'll see the degree sign more often than not to signify a diminished chord.
- Dominant Chords. Dominant chords come one way: letter/number. It's always C7 for a C dominant chord. Dominant chords sometimes come in other varieties, but they always adhere to the letter/number rule (C9, C11, C13), which makes them easy to spot.
- Augmented Chords. Augmented chords always follow the syntax C+. The + symbol appears after the root.

When you encounter any symbol, it's up to you as the chord player to make up your own chord voicing on your instrument. If you play piano or guitar, knowing how to play any major, minor, diminished, augmented, or dominant chord on your instrument is going to save your life when you encounter lead sheets. If you play jazz, this is standard fare.

Guitar Chord Diagrams

Another element you may see in lead sheets (or even in most popular music editions) is the inclusion of guitar chord diagrams. A guitar chord diagram instructs the guitar player exactly how to play each chord, using a gridlike system representing the six strings and a section of four or five frets. (See **FIGURE 20-2**.)

FIGURE 20-2 Guitar Chord Diagram

D Major

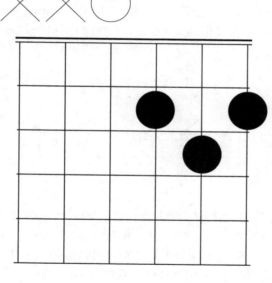

In addition to the typical chord symbols, guitar chord boxes are written above the symbols. If you don't play guitar, they won't mean much to you. If you do play guitar and find these symbols useful, look for the phrase "Piano/Vocal/Guitar" on the cover of any book or music sheet before you buy. Those editions contain the chord boxes. Of course, you're not locked into those particular voicings; they are merely suggestions. If you can play a better voicing of any chord listed, go right ahead.

Chord Rhythm

In a lead sheet, the chord symbols do not indicate rhythms for the duration of the chord the way that traditional notation does. Although they give you the ability to play any chord voicing you feel like, there is one glaring omission: rhythm! How long do you hold the chords and how many times do you strike them? This is a gray area. Typically, chord rhythm falls into two styles: vague and specific.

Vague Chord Rhythm

In this style of chord writing, all the composer gives you is the chord symbol floating above the melody line. This style is vague, but it's not empty. The chord symbols line up over specific beats in the melody. They don't just float meaninglessly. The duration of the chord is based on the meter and the placement of the chords over the melody. (See **FIGURE 20-3**.)

FIGURE 20-3 Vague Chord Rhythm

In **FIGURE 20-3**, there are four chords—one per measure. Each of the chords is lined up over the first beat of each bar. Since this example is in $\frac{4}{4}$ time, each chord will last for four beats and then change. In this style of chord notation, a written chord is "kept alive" until another chord symbol comes along to take its place.

If the chord changes in the middle of the measure, the chord will be aligned over a different beat, as shown in **FIGURE 20-4**. In the second bar, the chord is over the second beat, which is where it becomes active. In the third bar, there is a chord change each beat. Accordingly, each chord is lined up over the first, second, third, and fourth beats.

FIGURE 20-4 Changing Chords Mid-Measure

Free Reign

In this style of chord notation, you are able to choose how long to hold the chord, but there's no indication of how many times to strike it. If the chord lasts for four beats, what are you to do for those four beats? In this style: anything you want. You are allowed to create whatever rhythm you feel like—as long as it lasts for the total number of beats the chord rings for. Although freedom is wonderful, it may be easier for the player to have a bit more information. More specific chord rhythms exist for this very purpose.

Specific Chord Notation

Occasionally, you find a layer of rhythmic notation with the chord symbols. This rhythmic notation looks different than traditional rhythms. The rhythms are displayed as a "rhythm slash," which resembles a crushed note (see **FIGURE 20-5**). The rhythms themselves are similar to traditional rhythms; they just look like someone squished them in a press. These rhythms are displayed above the melody line, below the written chord symbols. In this style of notation, you can tell exactly how long to play each chord and what rhythm to play them with. You find this with lead sheets when a specific rhythm is needed.

FIGURE 20-5 Rhythmic Notation

Building a Bass

Now that the melody and chords are solidified, let's look briefly at how a bass player might look at a lead sheet. The bass can play a very simple role if it chooses. All a bass player needs to do, at a minimum, is play the root of each chord as they go by. They do this by following the written chord symbols and playing the root of each chord (C for a C chord, etc.). For a simple lead sheet, the bass may play something like what's shown in **FIGURE 20-6**.

FIGURE 20-6 Bass Line

Original Lead Sheet

Bass Part Constructed From Chord Symbols

Yes, it's quite simple, and yes, Jaco Pastorius could do so much more. Part of playing bass is learning how to construct bass lines from standard chord symbols. This is beyond the scope of this book, but what you should understand is how this simple lead sheet can give so many disparate pieces of information to so many different players with such a simple visual system. Viva efficiency!

Chord Charts

Apart from the standard lead sheets discussed already, there is one subset of lead sheets that is found in keyboard, guitar, and bass music, especially in jazz and show music: the chord chart. A chord chart is basically a lead sheet minus the melody. Chord charts are used most often in jazz and show music.

As you can see in **FIGURE 20-7**, the melody is missing. In its place is the rhythmic slash notation you learned about earlier. These rhythms tell you how to play the chord symbols written above the staff. The chord symbols haven't changed at all. Thankfully, these are somewhat standard. Piano and guitar can read the written chords easily and a bass player can make up or "walk" a bass line based on the chord symbols. If you ever play in a jazz band or play show music, you probably will encounter this style of notation.

FIGURE 20-7 Chord Chart

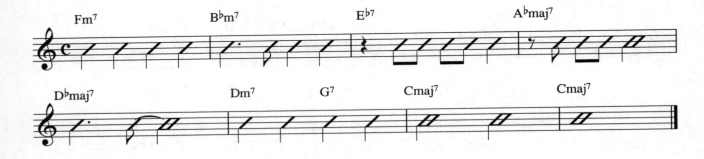

How to Simplify a Lead Sheet

This last section of the book deals more with jazz and contemporary music than anything else. In folk and popular music, the chords tend to be major and minor chords with an occasional dominant. In jazz music, the chords can be quite elaborate. At first, you may think to yourself, "I don't know enough chords." Luckily for you, no matter what you're looking at, any chord can be broken down into four main categories: major, minor, dominant, and diminished/augmented.

Tall Chords

Jazz music makes use of "extensions" on chords. Extensions are added notes to the top of the chords. Typically these extensions are intervals of a ninth, eleventh, and thirteenth. Extensions can also be any combination. The good news about extensions is that you don't have to play them. Extensions provide a more colorful harmony, one that is more "jazz"-like. However, the basic chord still stays the same. For example, if you see C major thirteenth, it's in the family of C major seventh, and you can play that instead. The same holds true for any extended chord:

- Cm11 = C minor 7
- C13 = C7 (C dominant)

This is the case no matter how elaborate the chord is. Here is a scary example:

- E7 ♭9 #9 ♭5 #5 ♮13

That's an actual chord! Disregard everything after the E7 and simply play an E7 chord. Even though the chord asks for more, by playing less you're not playing anything wrong—you're just playing a simpler harmony. This works with any jazz chord you can think of. When in doubt—simplify.

Now, no matter what you encounter, you can play something. In time, learn how to play every chord. In the meantime, play something.

Congrats! You made it! If you retained everything from this book you are well on your way to a degree in music. There is a lot of information in this book. Keep it handy; come back often, as there are many years of study here for you. Good luck in your music.

Appendix A
Scale and Chord Reference

Chord Review

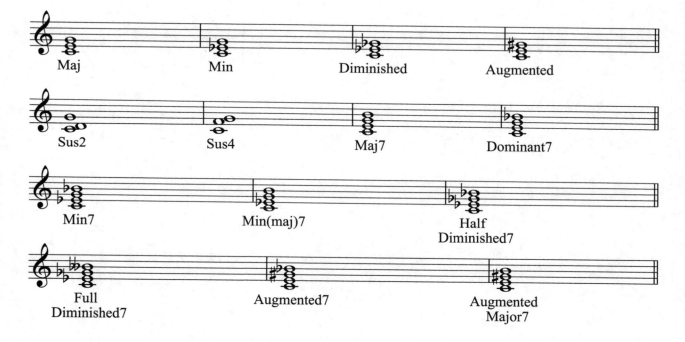

Scale Review

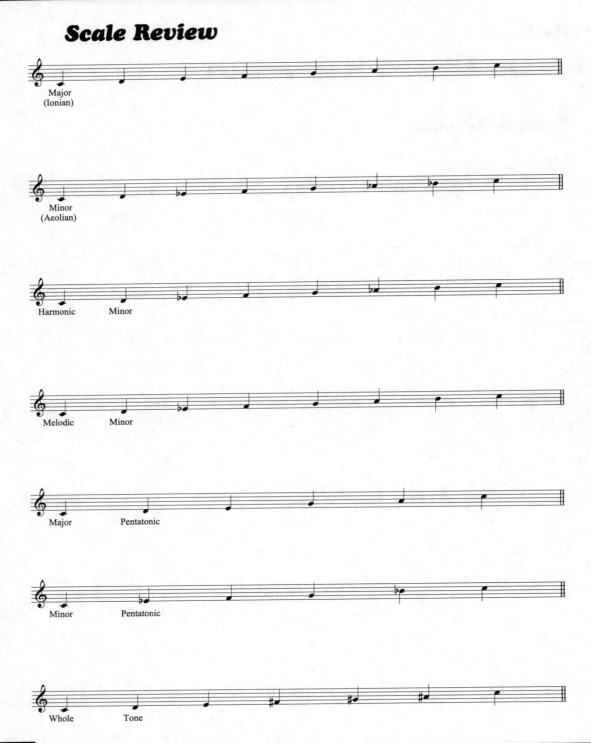

Major
(Ionian)

Minor
(Aeolian)

Harmonic   Minor

Melodic   Minor

Major   Pentatonic

Minor   Pentatonic

Whole   Tone

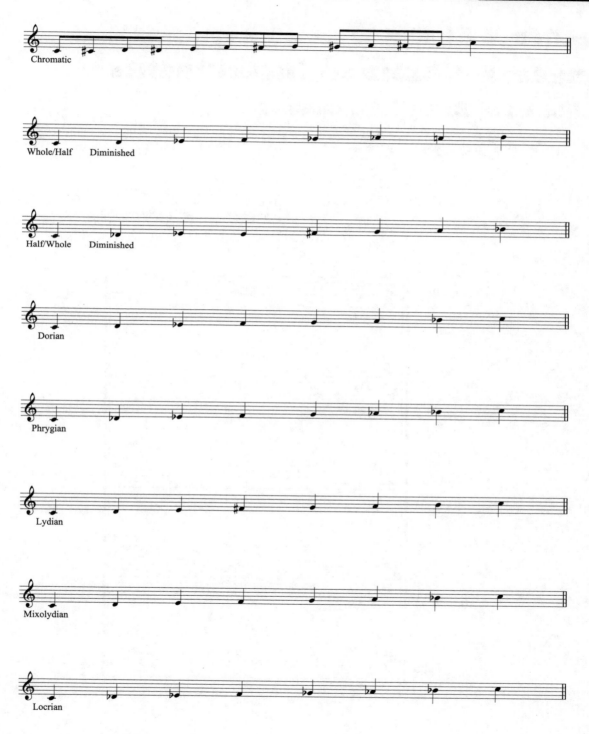

Ranges of Common Instruments

Ranges of Brass Instruments

Written Pitches

Lowest Note

Highest Practical Note -
Professional Range Can Be Higher

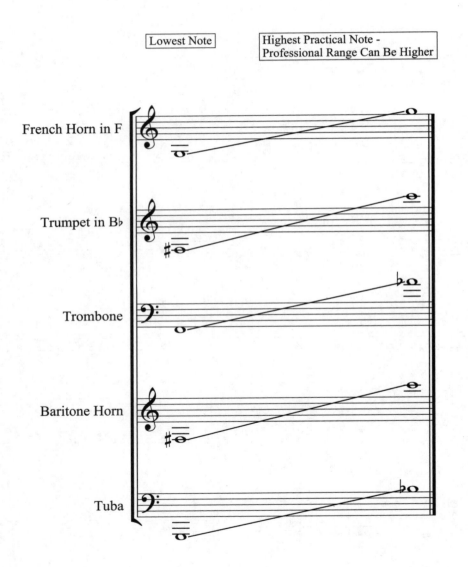

Ranges of String Instruments

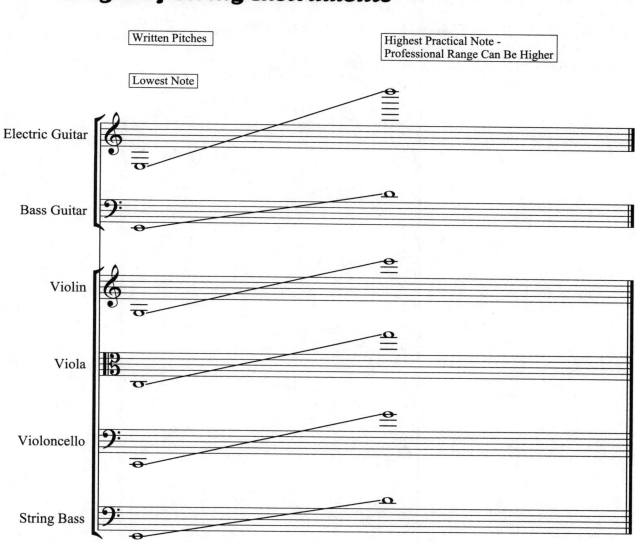

Written Pitches

Lowest Note

Highest Practical Note - Professional Range Can Be Higher

Electric Guitar

Bass Guitar

Violin

Viola

Violoncello

String Bass

Ranges of Wind Instruments

Written Pitches

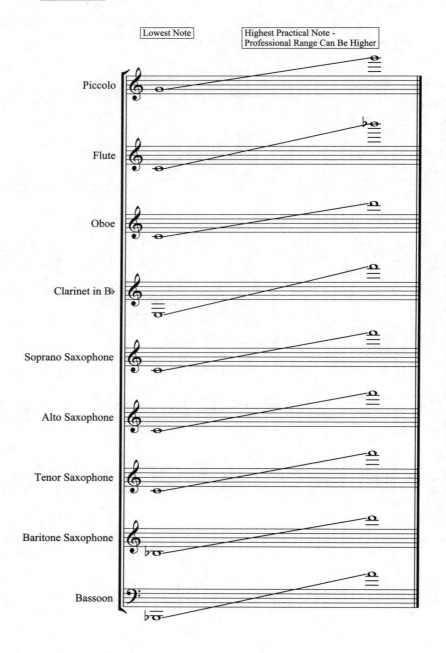

Lowest Note

Highest Practical Note -
Professional Range Can Be Higher

Piccolo

Flute

Oboe

Clarinet in B♭

Soprano Saxophone

Alto Saxophone

Tenor Saxophone

Baritone Saxophone

Bassoon

Ranges of Voices

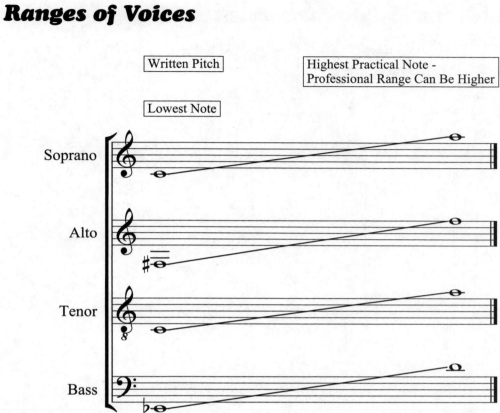

Written Pitch

Highest Practical Note -
Professional Range Can Be Higher

Lowest Note

Soprano

Alto

Tenor

Bass

Solutions to Exercises

Interval Quiz, Solution to Figure 13-12, page 167

FIGURE APPENDIX C1

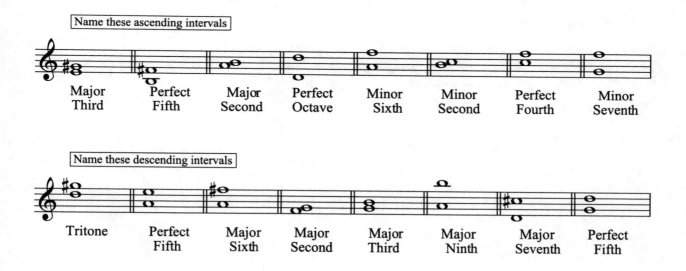

Trumpet Transposing, Solution to Figure 19-9, page 253

FIGURE APPENDIX C2

French Horn Transposing, Solution to Figure 19-10, page 252

FIGURE APPENDIX C3

Alto Saxophone Transposing, Solution to Figure 19-11, page 253

FIGURE APPENDIX C4

Index

We Have
EVERYTHING®
on Anything!

With more than 19 million copies sold, **the Everything® series** has become one of America's favorite resources for solving problems, learning new skills, and organizing lives. Our brand is not only recognizable—it's also welcomed.

The series is a hand-in-hand partner for people who are ready to tackle new subjects—like you!

For more information on the Everything® series, please visit *www.adamsmedia.com*

The Everything® list spans a wide range of subjects, with more than 500 titles covering 25 different categories:

Business	History	Reference
Careers	Home Improvement	Religion
Children's Storybooks	Everything Kids	Self-Help
Computers	Languages	Sports & Fitness
Cooking	Music	Travel
Crafts and Hobbies	New Age	Wedding
Education/Schools	Parenting	Writing
Games and Puzzles	Personal Finance	
Health	Pets	

SOFTWARE LICENSE AGREEMENT